GOOD

The Complete

CATS,

A-to-Z Guide for When

BAD

Your Cat Misbehaves

HABITS

Alice Rhea

Another idea from becker & mayer!

A FIRESIDE BOOK

Published by Simon & Schuster

New York   London   Toronto   Sydney   Tokyo   Singapore

OUACHITA TECHNICAL COLLEGE

FIRESIDE
Rockefeller Center
1230 Avenue of the Americas
New York, NY 10020

Designed by Richard Oriolo

Manufactured in the United States of America

10 9 8 7 6

Library of Congress Cataloging-in-Publication Data
Rhea, Alice.
Good cats, bad habits: the complete A-to-Z guide for when your cat misbehaves/Alice Rhea.
p.   cm.
Includes index.
1. Cats—Training—Encyclopedias. 2. Cats—Behavior—Encyclopedias. I. Title.
SF446.R48   1995
636.8'0887—dc20   95-32200
ISBN 0-684-81113-8

F
146
R48
995

Contents

Acknowledgments

This book would not have been possible without the friendship of Ken McKim, D.V.M., Greentree Animal Hospital, and Grady Shelton, D.V.M., Feline Retrovirus Referral Service. I am indebted to each of them for twelve years of excellent veterinary care for my dogs and cats, for sharing their knowledge of veterinary medicine with me, for providing resource materials on many subjects throughout the years, and for proofreading my manuscript. I am grateful for their friendship and caring.

I am also indebted to the judges, officers, instructors, breeders, and exhibitors of The International Cat Association (TICA) for sharing their friendship and their knowledge of cats with me. I learned more about cats during my first year of showing cats than in all my previous experience as a cat lover.

I am also indebted to J. B. Reynolds and Karl Kunkle, former editors of the *Snoqualmie Valley Reporter*, for nurturing my desire to write and for their help in improving my skills.

**To my husband, Dale T. Rhea,
without whose constant support and encouragement
nothing would be possible**

Introduction

Welcome to the World of Cats

Your cat is already trained to come when called, although you probably don't realize it. Doesn't your cat come running every time you operate the can opener? Cats *can* be taught to use the scratching post, stay off the counters, and come when called, but they are so smart they have people convinced that they cannot be trained. In fact, most cats have their owners quite nicely trained. They eat only the most expensive gourmet foods, which *you* prepare at 4:00 A.M.; they saunter across the countertops, lie in the middle of the newspaper story you are trying to read, and walk across your face in the middle of the night. In short, cats are so smart that they are able to get away with the most atrocious behavior because of the mistaken belief that they cannot be taught civilized manners.

While few people have the interest or the time to train their cat as well as they might a dog, most do want a cat who is a well-mannered companion.

Cats do not need to defer to a pack leader in order to survive. As solitary hunters, cats are not predisposed to submit to a dominant leader. However, they do enjoy the physical and social benefits of living in a colony, and they do form loving bonds with their people. They understand that in order to remain in the colony (your home) and enjoy your love and affection, they must conform to some basic rules of behavior. Understanding how cats interact with their environment and with each other helps in learning how to get them to do what you want.

The basic principles of cat psychology based on a cat's natural instincts and methods of learning are used to train your cat to live in harmony in your household.

Throughout the book I frequently recommend neutering your

cat—so often, in fact, that you might think that is all you have to do in order to have a well-behaved cat. In many cases, that is true. Most sexually motivated behaviors of cats are annoying, and neutering eliminates these behaviors. Neutering also makes most cats calmer and more loving toward their owners. Unless you are using your cat in a controlled breeding program, there is no good reason not to neuter him, and many good reasons to do so. Your veterinarian will be happy to supply you with a list of medical reasons for neutering your cat.

I hope this book will help you understand and enjoy the behaviors that are unchangeable feline activities. I hope you learn how to redirect your cat's excess energy into acceptable channels and to correct any real behavior problems so you can live in peace and harmony with your lovely creature(s).

Every year thousands of beautiful, healthy, loving cats are put to death in animal shelters across our country simply because nobody wants them. Many of these cats once had homes but because of some unacceptable behaviors have landed in the shelter. Many people do not understand why cats do the things they do or how to make them stop undesirable activities. Attempts to correct the cat's annoying behavior are unsuccessful and leave the cat confused and upset, and their people frustrated and angry.

Pets are surrendered to animal shelters in the belief that other homes will be found for them. The sad fact is that most of the animals that are sent to shelters end their lives there. Whether the shelter is run by the city, the county, or a private charity, there simply is not enough room to take in all the stray, abandoned, and surrendered pets. Even the so-called no-kill shelters have limited room, and once these shelters are full, applicants are turned away. The cats who can't find a home in a no-kill shelter are either abandoned to fend for themselves or taken to another shelter. When that shelter becomes overcrowded, the excess animals are killed. Shelters use a humane method of killing these unwanted animals—if any premature death can be called humane—and we politely call it euthanasia to make it easier to accept.

If a cat is dumped in a rural area to fend for himself, he may manage to scrape out some sort of short, miserable existence, but at best he will be lonely, frightened, cold, hungry, and in constant danger. His life expectancy becomes very short. A cat stands a much better chance in a shelter where, if not adopted, at least he will have food and shelter until he is gently put to death.

I also hope I can convince you to have your cat neutered or spayed, so he or she will be a better companion, enjoy a longer, healthier life, and will not produce kittens that will add to society's burden of having too many pets and two few homes.

Good Cats, Bad Habits provides clear, concise solutions to all the major and *minor* bad habits your cat might develop. It is structured in an easy-to-use A–Z format, so a solution to a specific problem can be found quickly. This format lists various behaviors alphabetically for easy reference. Each solution will provide *you* with an understanding of why *your* cat is behaving as he is, and the technique to be used right then and there to make him stop. All of the solutions are based on the understanding of why cats do what they do and how you can redirect them to do what you want.

The appendix is an expanded explanation of how to clip claws, how to introduce a new kitten to your home, and how to eliminate problems associated with the litter box.

Behaviors such as aggressive biting and other aggressive actions are not described in this book. Any aggressive behavior can potentially be very dangerous to other pets or humans, and the cat owner should seek professional help. Cats who were not handled by humans when they were young do not understand that humans can provide food, shelter, protection, and love. When cornered by these large creatures (humans), they behave as they would with any predator—they fight for their freedom. The same is true of cats who have been abused. They have learned that humans are their enemies. Scratches and bites inflicted by an angry or terrified cat can be very serious and require medical treatment. If you are determined to keep a feral cat—one who has not learned about humans—or if you want to reeducate a cat who has been abused, ask your veterinarian to recommend a professional to guide you.

It is essential that you be the top cat in the colony (your household), or your cat will ignore your wishes. At the same time, cats do not respond well to force. Punishment, such as hitting or yelling at them, will eventually cause them to avoid you, rather than stop their unwanted behavior. Physical correction, such as squirting them with water, is used only to startle them, not as a punishment.

While cats do not necessarily seek to please the top cat in the colony, they must not *displease* that individual if they wish to remain in the colony. Therefore, they don't want you to be angry at them and will try to remember what displeases you. They like quiet and solitude and will try to avoid behaviors that cause loud noise and disharmony.

Cats learn from immediate results: If your cat sinks her claws into the fabric of your velvet love seat and finds the sensation pleasing, she will continue to use the love seat as a scratching post. If your cat has a startling, unpleasant experience when she starts to scratch the love seat, such as a loud noise or a squirt from a spray bottle, she will learn not to do it again.

Be observant Watch your cat's ears, eyes, tail, and body posture as he goes through his day. A tall, waving tail and bouncing step display joy, while a horizontal, twitching tail expresses displeasure or preparation for pouncing upon his prey. Listen to your cats when they vocalize with each other and with you. A query of "Mmmert?" may say "Hello, how are you," or "What's for dinner," while "Mmmort!" means "You're standing on my tail!" With a little practice you will be able to discern when your cat is saying he needs to go to the bathroom but the litter box is not available or is not clean enough to suit him.

Be vocal Your cat's hearing is highly developed. While she may not recognize you if you are wearing a hat when you usually go bareheaded, she will recognize your voice if you speak to her. Explain things to your cat. Even though you may not think she understands the words you say, she will recognize your voice and the tone you are using. Loud, sharp words are used to stop unwanted behavior, while soft, gentle words are used to praise or calm your cat.

Be consistent You must correct your cat every time she acts out a bad habit. If you give in some of the time, your cat learns that you are not serious and bad habits will be even more difficult to correct.

Be aware Observe your cat's body language and learn to recognize when she is about to pounce. This will enable you to stop your cat's inappropriate behavior before she gets started.

Be timely When your cat misbehaves, you must correct her immediately. One minute after she stops the behavior is too late. Punishment will only confuse her.

Be gentle Correct your cat as mildly as possible. Forceful treatment only fosters resentment in your cat.

Be sincere Tell your cat, "Oh, what a good kitty," when she uses her scratching post. Even if she does not understand the words, she can hear the approval in your voice.

Be tolerant Try to understand the situation from your cat's point of view. Your cat needs your love and affection, play, exercise, and quiet time as much as she needs good food and a warm place to sleep. Try to meet her emotional needs as well as her physical needs.

Be creative Try to find an alternative to the unwanted behavior. For instance, when you make her stop scratching the love seat, take her over and place her on the scratching post. If you don't want her to wrestle with your arm, provide a large stuffed toy and show her how to play with it.

Be patient Learning new behavior takes time. Don't be discouraged if it takes longer than you expected to eliminate unwanted behaviors. Think about how long your cat has been doing things the way he wants and expect to take at least that much time to teach him to do them your way.

Be considerate of yourself You have a right to a peaceful and orderly household. Don't let your cat's natural reluctance to change defeat you. It is natural to feel frustrated and angry, but don't allow those feelings to interfere with your calm approach to retraining your cat. Remember that the anger and frustration will be replaced by feelings of satisfaction and joy as your cat learns to behave in ways that please you.

Be available Cats love routine. Plan regular times to spend with your cat—playing, grooming, or just watching TV together.

Be flexible Cats are intuitive creatures—accept that the cat is sensitive to your needs, too. Maybe she is sitting in the middle of your project because you need a break. Stop working and refresh yourself with a few minutes of visiting or playing with your cat friend.

Health and diet Inappropriate behavior can be a signal that your cat has a medical problem. Have regular veterinary checkups and follow your veterinarian's advice.

Remember that you are training your cat so she will be an enjoyable member of your household—not to intimidate her or display your power over her. Training her with love will accomplish your desires and help seal the bonds of affection between you. Keep corrections as quiet and mild as possible. Cats have very keen hearing, and it is not necessary to shout to get their attention.

How to Use This Book

This book is designed so you can quickly locate the section on your problem and find the solution. Entry headings are arranged alphabetically and appear in bold type in a screened panel for easy reference. In most cases, each entry includes the following:

1. The name of the behavior.

2. A description of the behavior, so you can quickly see if this is what your cat is doing.

3. *Why is my cat doing this?* This section explains the instinctual and/or environmental reason for your cat's behavior. This helps you understand that the behavior is perfectly natural from the cat's perspective and needs changing, but not punishment.

4. *How can I make her/him stop?* This tells you what to do immediately.

5. *What to say and do.* This tells you in detail how to make your cat stop what he is doing and start doing it your way. This section also provides suggestions to make it easier for your cat to conform to your desires.

6. *Why this works.* An explanation of why the solutions presented are effective will help you understand the logic of your actions and encourage you to continue your efforts.

7. *Preventative tips.* These explain ways you can prevent problems and ways to fulfill your cat's needs so unwanted behaviors won't be repeated.

Training Tools

There are eight essential tools for proper cat training that will be mentioned throughout the book as methods to correct various behaviors. To avoid duplication, for each alphabetical entry the tool will be mentioned simply by the tool's name and highlighted in italics. It is very important that you understand how to use each tool and be consistent!

Tool #1: Gentle voice and petting Use praise and petting to calm your cat when she has been overexcited, or when she is displaying correct behavior that you want to encourage—for instance, when she is using the scratching post or the litter box. Talk to her. Explain what is going on, even if you don't think she understands your words. Speak softly and quietly to your cat while you slowly stroke her to show your love and approval. Using the palm of your hand, softly stroke your cat from the top of her head to the base of her tail. Scratch gently under her chin, on her chest, and behind her ears. Vigorous scratching or quick patting will only excite her even more. Stroking your cat conveys your feelings of love and appreciation. This bond of trust and affection forms the basis of your relationship.

Tool #2: Sharp clap Clap your hands sharply to make a startling "smack!" sound. This noise surprises your cat into stopping whatever he is doing, such as jumping up on the counter while you are preparing dinner. Use the sharp clap when you can't reach your cat to relocate him, or when don't want to touch him—for instance, when you are working with food or washing dishes, or when your cat is in an area you don't want to spray with water, or when the spray bottle is not handy.

Tool #3: Spray bottle A simple plastic spray bottle filled with plain water can be used to interrupt unwanted behaviors without physical force, and in cases where you don't want your cat to know you are causing the discomfort. The spray bottle is used to stop behaviors for which there is no acceptable substitute, such as jumping on counters (if he is scratching the couch, the acceptable substitute is his scratching post). The spray bottle makes the behavior—getting on the counter—disagreeable without linking the unpleasantness directly to you. Not knowing where the water came from will help convince your cat that the countertop is not a good place. The spray bottle is also used to stop inappropriate behavior, such as attacking your feet. After squirting him to make him stop his attack, spend some time playing with him with a ball or other toy.

Set the nozzle so it emits a hefty spray, not an ineffective mist or a strong stream of water that might injure your cat's eye. The spray should be robust enough to startle the cat, but not strong enough to cause injury if the cat suddenly turns and receives a blast in the face.

The spray bottle is not effective with all cats. Some cats do not mind being squirted. Long-haired cats simply may not notice they are being sprayed, but even some short-haired cats seem impervious to being squirted.

Tool #4: Magazine toss Use a lightweight magazine such as *People* or *TV Guide*. When held by the spine and tossed in a level trajectory, it makes scary noises as it flutters through the air and lands near your cat. It startles her and makes her stop what she is doing. Like the spray bottle, the magazine toss is used when you want your cat to connect the unpleasant noise with his behavior, rather than with you. The magazine toss is especially useful when your cat is in an area where you don't want to use the spray bottle, such as near the couch or drapes, or for use with cats who don't mind being sprayed with water. Do not try to hit your cat with the magazine. You just want to startle her—not inflict pain.

Tool #5: Carrier A cat carrier is normally used to transport your cat during car and plane trips, and to confine him when he can't be watched. The carrier also provides a safe haven for your cat, giving him a private space all his own inside your house. Equipped with his familiar bedding and small soft toy, the carrier serves your cat as a comfortable "safe place" when he travels with you. While cats enjoy small, confined areas of privacy, getting an adult cat used to being confined in his carrier takes time and training. This is explained in detail in the section Carrier, won't get in.

Tool #6: Hiss The hissing noise is a sound cats make to each other as a near-to-final warning that wrong behavior is about to be punished. Hissing at your cat lets her know she has seriously violated your rules. Hold your front teeth together, part your lips, and forcefully expel air from your mouth, making a sound like "Sssst!" All cats recognize this signal and will, at least, stop and look around to see what is making that noise. If the hiss is repeated several times, most cats will move away from the sound.

Tool #7: Grooming Grooming is the most effective way to build love and trust between you and your cat. Cats communicate love and trust among themselves through mutual grooming. By spending fifteen to twenty minutes a day of quiet time with your cat, you can teach the cat to trust you and to enjoy the physical pleasure of being combed and brushed. Stroke the comb or brush gently from the top of the cat's head to the end of his tail. Comb or brush upward on the throat and chin, and down the chest and belly. Take care to stroke in the direction the hair grows, and don't pull the hair.

Tool #8: Shaker can When rolled or dropped, an aluminum pop can, filled with a few pieces of gravel, makes a scary rattling noise that frightens your cat, making her stop what she is doing. The shaker can is an excellent tool for scaring your cat away from forbidden places when you aren't in the room. The cans are arranged so they roll or fall off when your cat touches them, making a clatter. Cats hate loud noises, and this one has the advantage of being unconnected to people. It seems to the cat that the object she touched made the awful noise, and helps convince her to stay away from it even when you aren't home.

**Run the comb or brush down the cat's back from
the top of his head to the base of his tail.**

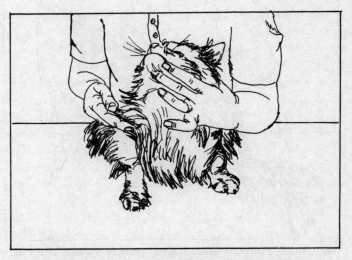

**Using your free hand, gently raise his chin and
comb his throat and chin in an upward motion.**

This is a sensuous pleasure for your cat. Most cats
will hold up their heads to have their throat and
chin groomed, and will lean into the comb or brush
to extract maximum pleasure from the experience.

With the palm of your hand, gently stroke the cat
from the top of his head to the base of his tail.

Use both hands to pet your cat. Stroke his back with one hand and scratch his neck and ears with the other.

These tools are the foundation of a well-trained cat, especially when used *together*. You will combine the trust and calmness you gain from the petting and grooming sessions, along with your cat's understanding that you are top cat and that he is in your territory. Using this combination, you can make it easy for your cat to learn to do what you want with good grace. For example, if your cat is about to scratch the couch, you can stop her with a simple "No, Sarah!" and a *sharp clap*. Then, as you carry her and place her feet on the scratching post, you can calm her with the same gentle voice and petting you shared previously. The shaker can is used to reinforce your wishes even when you can't be in the same room as your cat. For instance, placing shaker cans on top of the toilet tissue roll so they will clatter to the floor if the cat plays with the tissue will discourage your cat from unrolling the paper even when you are not at home.

Cat

Problems,

from A to Z

Aggression, after being chased

We were ready to leave on vacation, and when we tried to catch Aurora to take her for boarding, she acted like she wanted to fight us. We chased her into a corner, and she turned around and arched her back and hissed at us. Her fur was standing on end and her ears were laid back and she looked serious. We had to leave her alone until she seemed calm. Is there something wrong with her?

Why is my cat doing this? Aurora was ready to defend herself and you were smart to allow her time to cool off and recognize you. Aurora was displaying fear aggression and, in that highly agitated state, probably did not recognize you as friends. Had you attempted to pick her up, she very likely would have bitten and scratched in an attempt to escape. Part of her reaction was because she sensed your anxiety. Aurora didn't like the bustle caused by the last-minute rush to finish packing and get out of the house. Her perfectly natural reaction to the agitation in the household was to hide— a survival instinct that has served cats well through the centuries. No doubt Aurora's anxiety was increased when she sensed you were displeased because you couldn't find her when you were ready to leave. Being chased and cornered was the last straw, and Aurora decided that she was in serious trouble and needed to defend herself. Cats who feel trapped and threatened will turn and face their chaser. In order to appear larger, they turn their bodies sideways, arch their backs and tails, and puff out their fur. The vulnerable ears are laid flat against the skull to make them less exposed to bites.

How can I make her stop? This is normal behavior that may happen any time Aurora feels frightened and trapped. The way to prevent triggering her aggressive reaction to fear is to change the way *you* prepare for your trip.

What to say and do Put Aurora, with her food, water, litter box, and carrier, in a quiet room, such as the guest bathroom, an hour or so before it is time for you to leave. This places Aurora out of the way of the traffic and relieves you of the anxiety of locating her and her carrier at the last minute.

When you are ready to go, calmly enter the bathroom and say in a cheerful voice, "Okay, Aurora, are you all ready to go on vacation?" Put her in the carrier and take her out to the car.

The other way to keep Aurora calm is to put her in her carrier and place the carrier in a quiet spot before you start dashing around getting ready to leave. If your car is in the garage or a sheltered spot where the temperature won't be too high or too low, you can go put her in her carrier in the car an hour or so before you leave.

Why this works Aurora is a nice cat and wouldn't dream of biting the hand that feeds her, but the combination of events surrounding your departure scared her out of her wits. Placing her in a quiet room, or in her carrier in a quiet spot, will keep her from being frightened.

Preventative tips Aurora probably already comes running whenever you run the can opener, open the refrigerator, or rattle her dry food. Use this method to call her before the excitement starts. It is very difficult to catch a cat when you are in a rush, and most cats will run if you chase them. Plan to have Aurora confined in a quiet place so all of you have a more pleasant beginning for your vacation.

Aggression, female

We have two young female cats who are sisters. They have lived together all their lives and have always played together. Suddenly they have started fighting. This is not the normal tussling they have always done—these fights are serious. We don't like the uproar in the house and we are afraid they will hurt each other. How can we make them stop fighting and be friends again?

Why is my cat doing this? One of the girls may have a medical problem. If Sadie or Sally is not feeling well, or has a painful sore, she may be trying to make the other cat leave her alone. If Sadie and Sally have not been spayed, one or both of them may have entered puberty, and they may be fighting simply because they feel out of sorts. A third possibility is that the aggression is being triggered by something outside the house. If their territory has been invaded by a dog or cat they can see but can't reach, the girls may be attacking each other in frustration.

How can I make her stop? Removing the cause of the problem will end the battles. Your veterinarian can help you determine if the cause is medical.

What to say and do Take Sadie and Sally to your veterinarian for checkups. Your veterinarian can tell you if one or both of them has a medical problem and recommend treatment. If the girls have not been spayed, your veterinarian can also advise you on the appropriate time to have this done.

If your veterinarian can find no medical reason for Sadie and Sally to be at odds with one another, look for signs that their territory has been invaded. Check for stains around the bottoms of outside doors and windows that indicate another cat has sprayed. Look for dog droppings in the yard and check for paw prints or broken plants in the flower beds near the house. Some people allow their dogs outside without supervision to relieve themselves, and they may not be aware that their dog is using your yard for his toilet and upsetting your cats. If you know the owner of the dog, tell her that her dog is not staying in his yard when she lets him out. This is a very delicate subject that requires a diplomat's touch to prevent a feud. Say, "Jane, are you aware that Kobuk is roaming around the neighborhood when you let him out in the evening? I'm worried that he will be hit by a car on this busy street." If your neighbors are responsible pet owners they will appreciate the information.

The alternative is to make your yard an unpleasant place for neighborhood dogs and cats to visit. Commercial repellents are available from pet stores. Apply these repellents around the perimeter of the yard and around the outside of the house.

If you see a dog or cat in your yard, step out the door and yell "Scat! Go home!" and clap your hands to make more noise.

Why this works Sadie and Sally had a good relationship, and once you remove the cause of the fights they will go back to being friends.

Preventative tips Any sudden change in behavior may signal a medical problem. Check with your veterinarian so you can catch problems early, while they are still treatable.

Aggression, male

Donnie came to us as a tiny kitten and fit right into our family. He has always been very friendly with our two older cats and with both of us. He has suddenly starting jumping on the two other cats, biting and swatting them. There doesn't seem to be any pattern to this bizarre behavior. In between attacks he is his normal, loving self, then without warning he will jump on one of the other cats. He has even bitten me once or twice. He didn't draw blood, but I'm worried that he is getting mean. Why is Donnie attacking the other cats?

Why is my cat doing this? Donnie sounds like he is outgrowing kittenhood and becoming an adolescent. The random, unpredictable attacks, which are undertaken without inflicting any damage, sound very much like mating behavior. Sexually intact males are ready to start breeding from about five months of age. This age varies widely among breeds, but a good rule of thumb is that the long, slender cats—Siamese, Oriental Shorthair, and Abyssinian types—have been known to exhibit breeding behavior as early as four months, with five months being a fairly common age for entering puberty. Medium-bodied cats such as Maine Coons, Ragdolls, and Norwegian Forest Cats generally become sexually mature at seven or eight months, and stocky or cobby cats, such as Persians and Exotic Shorthairs, may not show any interest in breeding until they are as old as two years.

The aggression shown in breeding does not have any anger behind it, which is why your other cats don't stay mad at Donnie for attempting to breed them. Usually sexually excited male cats simply wait for an opportunity, such as when the female has her back to him, before attempting to breed. The male grasps the female by the scruff of the neck to assist in positioning, but these bites are generally not painful and usually do not do any damage. Occasionally a very reluctant female may escape from a very determined male and lose a chunk of hair in the process.

How can I make him stop? The way to make Donnie stop attacking you and the other cats in the household, and consequently turn him into a calmer, more loving pet, is to remove the cause of the problem by having him neutered.

What to say and do Do Donnie the biggest favor of his life and have him neutered. Your veterinarian can give you a long list of the benefits Donnie will receive from being neutered. Neutered males make better pets. If they are neutered before they start spraying, they do not spray urine on furniture and walls in an effort to announce their sexual availability to females. They do not beat down the doors or claw or bash their way through the window or door screens in an effort to meet with neighborhood females who are in heat, and they do not get into fights with other toms over females. Even if you allow Donnie to go outdoors, he will stick closer to home and be less likely to get into territorial fights with other cats.

Preventative tips Have your cats neutered as soon as your veterinarian thinks they are old enough to have the surgery.

Aggression, toward dogs

We recently got a new kitten, and she is sweet and playful except when our dog is in the house. Tracy jumps out from behind things and attacks him, and when he retreats from her she chases him. Our well-trained dog does not fight with the kitten, but we would like them to be friends. Why does our kitten hate dogs? What can we do to make her behave when the dog is in the house?

Why is our kitten doing this? Observe the kitten carefully. Tracy may truly hate dogs, but kittens are not born hating or fearing other animals or people. If kittens have been well socialized—that is, frequently handled by humans while they were young—they should adapt to other animals fairly easily. After a brief get-acquainted period, assuming Bruno has behaved like the well-trained family member he is, Tracy should play with—or, at worst, ignore—him.

What to say and do It sounds like Tracy may be playing a kitten game called "ambush" with Bruno. Kittens love to play this game with each other, hiding behind things, crouching, switching their tails, then pouncing on an unsuspecting littermate when one wanders by. The kittens then roll and tumble and bite and scratch each other, and in general have a rousing good time. Although the game appears ferocious, kittens rarely injure one another, and at the end of the game they often settle down together for a nap. In the absence of littermates, kittens often substitute other species, such as the human or canine members of the family.

In any case, clip Tracy's claws so nobody gets injured while you are solving the problem.

To see whether this is a game or serious business, set up a scene where Tracy isn't hiding in ambush when Bruno enters the room. With another person to help you, sit with Tracy on your lap and stroke her and talk to her while your assistant brings Bruno into the room. Say, "Pretty Tracy, what a nice kitty you are. Aren't we lucky to have such a pretty kitten?" Have Bruno lie down and stay still and continue stroking and talking to Tracy. Say, "Oh, look, Tracy, here is your new friend, Bruno. Bruno loves Tracy. Bruno would love to be Tracy's friend."

After a few minutes, encourage Tracy to get off your lap, or stand up and put her on the floor. If Tracy growls or hisses at Bruno or struggles to get down or dashes over and attacks Bruno, use the *sharp clap* and say, "No, Tracy! We do not attack Bruno! Bruno lives here, too."

If Tracy does not immediately break off the attack, pick her up, put her in another room, and close the door. Be sure to let Tracy see and hear you before you attempt to pick her up. If she is seriously attacking Bruno, she may not realize that it is you who is grabbing her, and she may turn and scratch and bite you.

Try to reintroduce Tracy and Bruno using the techniques described in the section New Kitten, in the Appendix. There are cats who are so territorial that they will not tolerate another animal in "their" house, but this is unusual in a young kitten.

Why this works Young kittens do not know what species they are. If introduced early, kittens will make friends with almost any other animal it meets—dogs, hamsters, rabbits, birds, other cats, and so on. The important thing is early handling by humans and early, gentle introduction to other animals.

Preventative tip Always introduce new household members using the techniques in the section New Kitten, in the Appendix. Most kittens and cats are not eager to meet other animals and usually take a few days to get acquainted.

See also:
Ambushing
Appendix (Clipping Claws)

Aggression, toward other cats

My three-year-old cat attacks any other cat I bring into the house. We recently got a new kitten, thinking Jose would like to have company while we are at work, but he seems to hate her. Whenever he sees the kitten, Jose runs over and beats up on her. Why is he doing this? How can we make him stop?

Why is my cat doing this? It is perfectly normal for Jose to proclaim his status as top cat in the household. While cats do not live in packs as dogs do, cats who live in multicat households or in feral cat colonies establish a hierarchy. It is not uncommon for them to have occasional spats. A minor amount of growling, hissing, and ear boxing is likely to occur if a cat of lower status forgets her place. There will also be some discord if a new member is introduced to the household or colony.

What to say and do Jose may simply be telling the kitten that he is the boss of the furry household members. It is not unusual for cats and kittens who already live in the house to try to put a new member in her place.

Observe Jose and the kitten carefully to see if Jose is seriously beating up on the kitten or just trying to establish the pecking order. If Jose mildly smacks the kitten when she gets too close to him, or hisses or growls if she tries to join him in his favorite chair, he is likely just telling her who's the boss. He may also swat her at mealtime, literally shoving her face in the food.

The kitten's reaction is also important in trying to decide if there is a problem. If Jose's behavior is normal—hierarchical—the kitten should cringe or move away when he threatens her, but she should soon come back for more.

When the kitten tries to join Jose in his nap, pick her up and place her on a hand towel or small rug or blanket in another spot. Say, "That's Jose's place. He doesn't want company right now. Let's let Jose have his spot and we'll make a place over here for you. There now, isn't that nice?"

At dinnertime, place the cat's dishes at a distance from each other so Jose doesn't feel he has to compete for food. You may have to feed the kitten in another room until Jose gets used to having her in the house. If Jose continues to be unfriendly to the kitten, or if he is seriously attacking her, try reintroducing them. If Jose continues to attack the kitten after you use the techniques in the section New Kitten, in the Appendix, to try reintroducing them, use the *sharp clap*, and say, "No, Jose. The kitten lives here, too. You are going to have to learn to get along. I am the boss in the house and I want you to stop picking on the kitten."

Why this works These altercations often stop of their own accord once the cats decide on the household hierarchy. You can speed the process along by establishing ground rules.

Preventative tips There are a few unusual cats who simply will not tolerate another animal in the house. If Jose is one of these, you will have to resign yourself to having Jose as your only cat, or you will have to find him a home where he can be the only pet.

See also:
Appendix (New Kitten)

Alone, when you travel

My husband travels extensively with his job, and my recent promotion will require frequent travel. We are certain to have overlapping trips when both of us will be out of town at the same time. Our cat doesn't like riding in the car, even for short distances. He doesn't like strange places and he hates dogs. The last time we boarded him he had a fit on the trip over and he looked ill when we picked him up.

Why is my cat doing this? Sparky is likely upset about everything happening at once. Leaving him at home may be the answer.

What to say and do Many cats have such a good time at the kennel that they actually seem to look forward to their owners being out of town. There are many excellent boarding kennels exclusively for cats, and using one of these facilities will eliminate the dog problem.

But Sparky will probably be happier if you leave him at home and have a responsible person come in to care for him.

Many people have good results hiring a neighbor's youngster to come in and care for their pets, but unless you are certain that the young person is absolutely reliable, you are better off hiring a professional cat sitter.

Your veterinarian is a good source of candidates for the job. The veterinary technician may be willing to take care of cats before and after office hours. Often, veterinarians have interns—high school or college students interested in becoming veterinarians—who are interested in cat-sitting jobs. Interns work several hours a week for the veterinarian, learning the basics of good animal care. They are usually conscientious, reliable workers.

You'll need to decide how often the sitter needs to come see Sparky. Some cats are perfectly happy being fed and petted once a day. If Sparky eats only dry food, a single visit per day may be adequate. However, if Sparky eats canned food twice a day, he needs someone to provide fresh meals for him.

You may want to change Sparky's routine so he becomes accustomed to eating once a day. If you choose to do this, you should start well in advance of your next trip. Give him fresh water and a clean dish of fresh dry food once a day. Provide enough dry food so he can nibble throughout the twenty-four-hour period until the next feeding. Sparky may complain at the change in routine, but it is better to make changes one at a time.

Plan to have Sparky's caretaker visit your home in advance of your next trip so he or she and Sparky can become acquainted. Say, "Sparky, this is Jane. She will be taking care of you while Jim and I are out of town." Have the caretaker spend a few minutes petting or grooming Sparky so Sparky knows that you approve. Show the sitter where supplies and toys are kept and discuss any special needs.

Be sure to leave signed authorization for the pet sitter to have the pet treated at your veterinarian's office if a medical problem arises during your absence.

Why this works Most cats hate change, and the fewer changes they have to accept, the happier they are. Sparky will probably be most comfortable staying at home with his familiar napping spots, food and water dishes, litter box, and toys all in their usual places. He may be a little lonely during the hours he is used to being with you, but after a few trips he should become secure in knowing you will always return.

Preventative tips Get kittens used to riding in their carrier in the car before they are old enough to be resistant.

Ambushing

C harlie, our seven-month-old neutered male cat, is constantly leaping out from behind doors and furniture to scratch and bite the ankles of all three family members. Why is Charlie doing this? How can we make him stop?

Why is my cat doing this? While Charlie's bites and scratches are painful and should be stopped, he probably is just playing, and chances are very good that you can make him stop.

It is natural for kittens to hide in ambush with their eyes dilated and their tails twitching, waiting to pounce on an unsuspecting litter-mate. Charlie, having no littermates to stalk and leap upon, has substituted you, his human littermates.

How can I make him stop? The easiest way to stop Charlie's attacks is to provide him with a playmate of about the same age and size. After a brief get-acquainted period, Charlie will find the new kitten a much more satisfying playmate than humans and will direct his ambushes toward him.

What to say and do If it is not possible to have two kittens in the house, you need to take a two-step approach to the problem. Charlie needs an outlet for his playfulness. Draw Charlie out of his ambush position by rolling a Ping-Pong ball or a ball with a bell inside across the room before you enter or by using a kitty tease. Take a little extra time to play with Charlie and give him an outlet for his natural crouch-and-pounce needs.

In addition to the positive redirection for Charlie's ambushes, you may need to actively discourage him from pouncing on you.

Arm each family member with a *spray bottle* and have them carry it at all times. When Charlie springs from behind the couch and sinks his teeth and claws into your ankle, shout, "No! Charlie! Stop it!" or "Ouch, Charlie! That hurts!" and squirt him with the spray bottle.

During the training period, minimize the damage to your skin by clipping his claws.

Do not punish Charlie by hitting him or flicking him on the nose. Charlie's ambushes, while painful, are play. Hitting him may cause the playful aggression to become defensive aggression. Remember: only use discipline while the cat is acting out the unwanted behavior. Even thirty seconds is too long for a cat to associate what he *was* doing (attacking you) with what is happening to him *now* (getting an unpleasant squirt of water).

Why this works The combination of offering Charlie an outlet for his excessive playfulness and punishing his attacks on people should change his behavior within a few days or weeks.

Preventative tips Help Charlie act out his natural crouch-and-pounce instincts by playing with him. Balls that make noises, such as a jingle ball or a Ping-Pong ball on uncarpeted floors are very attractive to kittens. The game is more fun if you join in by making encouraging noises, such as "Go get it, Charlie! Get that ball! Pounce on it, Charlie!" While Charlie may not understand the words, he does know your tone of voice means you are playing together.

See also:
Appendix (Clipping Claws)

Bad breath

I know I can't expect my cat's breath to smell minty fresh, but Oreo really has bad breath. Her breath smells so bad we can't stand to have her near our faces. We're thinking of renaming her "Green Breath." Is there anything we can do to make her breath smell better?

Why is my cat doing this? Having bad breath isn't a behavior problem, but it is a problem—maybe more grave than merely being offensive to her people. Oreo may be in serious trouble. Foul breath may be a symptom of a medical problem.

How can I make her stop? You will have to do a little detective work to uncover the source of Oreo's foul breath. You will probably need to enlist the help of your veterinarian to aid in your search. While it is true that you can't expect your pets to have minty-fresh breath, foul breath indicates something is wrong. The odor may be caused by an abscessed or decayed tooth, gum disease, an oral tumor, kidney failure, a problem in her digestive tract, or some other medical condition. Cats also occasionally need to have their teeth cleaned. Your veterinarian should be examining Oreo's teeth and gums as a part of her regular checkup. The need for teeth cleaning varies from cat to cat, and cats who develop tartar on their teeth seem to do so regardless of what they are fed. Feeding Oreo dry food only may help in preventing tarter buildup on her teeth, but it will not completely eliminate it.

What to say and do First, take a look at what you are feeding Oreo. There are still some canned foods on the market with a very strong-smelling base, and after she eats one of these foods, a cat's breath just reeks! Smell Oreo's food, and if it smells strong, switch to another, less odoriferous brand. She may reject the new food at first, because cats do adore foods with a high odor—especially a strong, fishy one.

Another clue to bad breath can sometimes be found in the litter box. Often, the same problem that is causing the unpleasant breath also results in truly foul-smelling, and often loose, bowel movements. If Oreo's problem is not caused simply by her eating strong-smelling food, your veterinarian will want to know if Oreo is producing a normal stool.

If your veterinarian can find no physical cause for Oreo's bad breath, ask him to show you how to brush her teeth. Many cats enjoy excellent lifelong dental health with no help whatsoever, but most cats need at least an occasional professional cleaning, and some cats need to have their teeth brushed daily or weekly. There are toothpastes and mouthwashes made especially for dogs and cats, which are available from your veterinarian. Oreo might never learn to enjoy having her teeth brushed, but you might coax her to accept having you gently wipe off her teeth with a kitty dentifrice applied with a small cloth or a finger toothbrush. She might also allow you to flush her mouth with a mouthwash formulated to retard tartar on cats' teeth.

Do *not* use human toothpaste or mouthwash on Oreo. Get products made especially for cats from your veterinarian.

Why this works Early training in accepting oral hygiene procedures, combined with proper nutrition and routine veterinary care, will help ensure lifelong dental health. This is the basis for inoffensive breath.

Preventative tips Train kittens to accept dental procedures while they are young. During regular grooming sessions, gently insert your finger into her mouth and rub it around the outside of her teeth. She will quickly come to accept this procedure as a normal part of her pleasurable grooming. When she becomes accustomed to having you massage her teeth and gums, start using a small cloth or toothbrush during the session. (Special "finger toothbrushes" for pets are available in pet stores.) Finally, add kitty toothpaste to the brush or cloth.

If you feel silly about brushing Oreo's teeth, just don't tell anybody you are doing it.

Bathing, objecting to

Our veterinarian said that Rebel, our big black cat, has fleas and needs a flea bath. We got the special shampoo, but do not have any idea how to begin. The last time we tried to bathe Rebel he had a fit. How can we make him behave so we can give him a bath?

What to say and do Cats who actually enjoy being bathed are rare, but most will tolerate the process fairly well. The most important factor is your confidence that you can do it and that it is for Rebel's benefit. If you are not confident, have your veterinarian or a professional groomer bathe him. Ask your veterinarian about a sterile ointment for keeping soap out of Rebel's eyes, and what he thinks about using cotton balls to keep water out of his ears.

Unless your house is very warm, prepare Rebel's carrier or the bathroom so you can confine him with a small space heater until he is dry. Check every few minutes to make sure he does not overheat.

Some people find the kitchen or utility sink is the easiest place to bathe the cat. Gather the shampoo, a cream rinse, several towels, and a washcloth for cleaning his face and ears. If you have a spray attachment on your sink, put a rubber band around the handle so the water will flow through the sprayer rather than the faucet. Otherwise attach an auxiliary sprayer to the faucet, or place a plastic cup near the sink for rinsing. Have his favorite treat handy to reward him after the bath. Some people place a cage rack or screen in the sink to provide the cat with a firm footing.

Get a friend or family member to distract Rebel during the bath by talking to him and scratching his head and chin. They can also gently restrain him by placing a hand on his chest or shoulders to keep him from climbing out of the tub so you can use both hands for bathing.

Clip Rebel's claws, front and back, and comb him to remove loose hair. Say, "Oh, Rebel, we're going to have a nice bath and get rid of all those nasty old fleas. You are going to look so pretty and feel so good when we are through." Give him a small treat for being so good while you clipped his nails, and leave him alone while you adjust the flow and temperature of the bath water. The correct temperature should be comfortable on the inside of your wrist.

Start talking while you are adjusting the water and continue talking until you are finished and Rebel is settled in the drying area. Say, "We are almost ready to start your bath, Rebel. It is going to be so nice to be clean. Won't it be wonderful to get rid of those fleas? It will be nice not to itch anymore." Keep your voice light and cheerful. You are doing Rebel a big favor by ridding him of fleas.

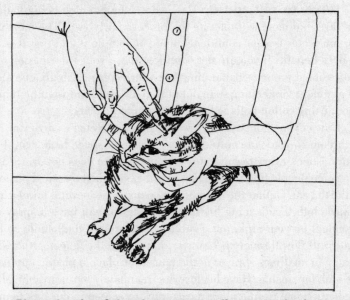

Place the tip of the shampoo applicator at the base of the cat's ear and apply a thin line of shampoo across the top of his head from ear to ear.

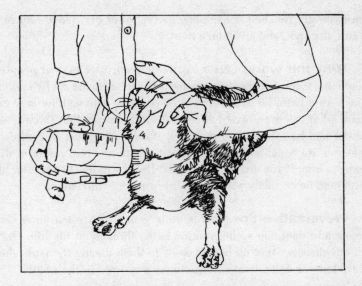

Raise his head and continue the shampoo line from the lower base of his ear, across his upper throat, to the opposite ear. This line of shampoo will prevent fleas from running onto the cat's face during the bath.

Leave the water running and place Rebel in the sink. Say, "Here we go, into the tub. Oh, what a brave kitty you are, Rebel. What a good boy to sit so nicely and let us bathe you. What a smart kitty to know we're helping you feel better." It doesn't matter what you say, but keep chatting with him about how brave and smart he is and how much better he is going to feel after the bath.

Draw a line around his head with the flea shampoo. Begin just behind his ears and across the top of his throat under his chin. This will keep the fleas from running into Rebel's eyes during the bath. Wet Rebel with the spray or by pouring water from the cup, add shampoo, and work up a lather. Spread the shampoo all over Rebel, including between his toes.

Do not clutch the cat. If Rebel is about to escape, simply lift him and place him back in the sink.

Be sure to rinse all the shampoo off. When you are absolutely sure you are finished, rinse once more. Towel dry, place him in a warm, dry spot, and give him a treat.

Why this works Cats are extremely sensitive to their people's emotions. If you believe that you are being mean to the cat by making him take a bath, he will feel your discomfort. Although he may not know what you are worried about, he will be aware that you are not serene and he will react to your lack of calm. You must be confident that you are capable of giving the cat a bath and that no harm will come to him. If you are convinced that Rebel will feel better after his bath (and he certainly will!), he will sense your conviction.

Preventative tips Start bathing your kitten when he is very young and continue giving routine baths throughout his life. Once kittens discover that no harm comes to them during the bath, they learn to relax and tolerate—sometimes even enjoy—their bath.

See also:
Appendix (Clipping Claws)

Bed, lying on

We have an adorable Persian who is perfect in every way, except she won't stay off the bed. We love her, but we hate having cat hair on the bed. She takes naps in her own bed, but she also wants to get on ours. How can we make her stop?

Why is my cat doing this? The bed must be the cat's idea of heaven. It is up off the floor, and cats love to be in elevated positions. It is warm, soft, and contains either the people Natasha loves or their scent.

What to say and do If cat hair on the bedspread is the only problem, the solution is fairly simple. Provide Natasha with her own space on the bed. Next time she is on the bed, pick her up and place a towel under her. Say, "Look, Natasha, here is your own special place on the bed. Isn't it nice to have your own place?" If the towel is in their preferred place, most cats will lie on it rather than the bedspread. Periodically laundering the towel is much easier than cleaning the bedspread, and the towels can be quickly whisked from sight when company arrives. Daily grooming will also dramatically reduce the amount of hair Natasha deposits, and Natasha will love the attention. Be sure to tell her how beautiful she is while you are grooming her. Say, "Natasha is such a pretty girl. What a beautiful coat you have. Oh, you are so soft."

If you do not want Natasha in bed with you at night, you have to be kind, firm, and persistent. If possible, place Natasha's box on top of the dresser or another piece of furniture so she can be up off the floor. Spend a few minutes petting and talking to Natasha just before bedtime to remind her how much you love her. When you are ready to get into bed, place Natasha in her box. Say, "Good night, Natasha," get in bed, and turn off the light.

If Natasha gets on the bed, say, "No, Natasha, I don't want you to sleep on my bed. I want you to sleep in your own bed," and put her back in her box.

You may have to get up many times and put Natasha back in her box. If she will not stay after repeated attempts, put her in another room. Say, "Natasha, I don't want you to sleep on my bed. If you won't stay off the bed, you'll have to sleep in the other room."

If Natasha cries to get back in, ignore her if you can. If her cries become too loud, or if she is scratching on the door, go to the door and say, "Natasha, be quiet. You can't sleep on my bed and you can't keep me up all night. Go to sleep."

If Natasha persists in yelling and scratching on the door, put her in her carrier. Say, "Natasha, you can't sleep in my bed. I don't want you to make so much noise, and I don't want you to damage the woodwork. If you can't be quiet, you'll have to sleep in your carrier."

If she continues to make so much noise you can't sleep, take the carrier into a remote part of the house. Try having Natasha in the bedroom again the next night and repeat the drill until Natasha gives in.

Why this works Cats love defined areas, such as a small box or a towel that contrasts with the bedspread, and will usually lie on or in the defined area rather than on the bed.

Banishment works because cats really do want to be near their people. As soon as they understand what is necessary in order to remain in the room and are convinced that you mean business, they usually will compromise with you.

Preventative tips Train your new kitten to sleep in her own bed. Remove her from your bed the first time, and every time, she gets on it. Be firm and consistent in not allowing her on your bed.

Begging at the table

We recently got a kitten who is very nice, except at mealtimes. We haven't had a peaceful meal since we got him. We feed him according to our veterinarian's recommendation, and he eats well, but when we sit down to eat, you would think we were starving him. He cries and jumps up on our laps and tries to steal the food from our plates. How can we make him stop?

Why is my cat doing this? Cats who live together usually do not display any territorial attitude about their food dishes. You will see each cat going from dish to dish, sampling a bite or two from each dish before settling down to eat a meal. It is also normal for these cats to allow their housemates to crowd them away from the dish they are eating from. Unless the crowder is new to the household or is a kitten whom the older cats think needs to learn some manners, the crowdee usually just moves to the next plate. He, in turn, crowds out the cat eating from that dish, and the displaced cat moves on to another dish. Cyrus is displaying what he believes to be common, good cat-manners.

How can I make him stop? All you need to do is teach Cyrus the table manners that are acceptable to people. This is easy—it just takes persistence and the ability to resist his pathetic starved-kitty routine. Your dinner may be disrupted for a few days, but he will soon learn not to pester you while you are eating.

What to say and do Change Cyrus's dinnertime to coincide with your own. Put his food in his regular eating spot just before the family sits down to dinner. You might consider giving him a good-quality canned cat food for dinner, at least during the training period. That way he has something interesting on his plate and may be less inclined to explore yours.

Never, never give Cyrus any food from the table. Once you give in and allow Cyrus the reward of people food for his bad behavior, you reinforce his efforts to eat from your table. When Cyrus comes to the table to beg, get up and carry him back to his dish. Say, "Here is *your* food, Cyrus. This is good stuff." Go back and sit down. When Cyrus comes back, repeat the exercise. "No, Cyrus, you can't beg at the table. You have your own food. This is where you eat." Go back and sit down.

If Cyrus is jumping on your laps or onto the table, simply pick him up and put him on the floor. Say, "No, Cyrus. We are having dinner now. You are not allowed on our laps or the table while we are eating." Some kittens are so smart they will learn this lesson after being removed from a lap or the tabletop as few as three times. Other kittens are like yo-yos and finally have to be shut out of the room so you can have dinner in peace.

If you have to put him in another room on your first, second, or third attempt at table-manner training, try allowing him in the room the following evening. He will eventually learn when he is welcome on your laps and when he is not.

Why this works Cats train kittens to stay away when they are not wanted by pushing them away. This is done when the kittens are being weaned, and the mother pushes them away with her hind feet. They eventually learn that they are not welcome at that dinner table, although their mother may spend a week or two convincing them that she means it.

Preventative tips Never allow your kitten to get in your lap or on the table while you are eating. It only takes one success—a kind word, petting, or some food—to convince her that she is welcome at mealtimes. Immediately place her on the floor every time she jumps up. Do not pet or feed her, and do not speak to her except to say "No!"

Birds and mice, bringing home

Samantha, our beautiful calico cat, catches birds and mice and brings them home. Sometimes she leaves the dead creatures in front of the door, and twice she "brought 'em back alive" and we had to figure out how to get a live bird or mouse out of the house. We hate to have her kill birds, and we also have heard that cats can get diseases from birds and mice. How can we make her stop killing things and bringing them home?

Why is my cat doing this? Samantha loves you. A rodent or bird placed in front of the door is Samantha's way of telling you how much she cares for you. One school of thought is that the cat has observed that you make no attempt to catch small game. Perhaps she feels sorry for your lack of hunting skill and is sharing her catch.

Samantha may be trying to teach you to hunt. Barn cats bring live prey back to the nesting area for the kittens to chase. Some believe the cat is attempting to teach her kittens the skills necessary to hunt for their own food. Others think the cat simply hasn't finished playing with the prey.

How can I make her stop? The only way to end the problem is to keep Samantha indoors. Veterinarians and other feline-care experts agree that cats live longer, healthier lives if they are kept indoors. Certainly no cat was ever killed by an automobile in his living room. Keeping Samantha indoors will also protect her from being lost, kidnapped, teased by children, and exposed to diseases and parasites. With all the advances in veterinary medicine in recent years, there are still diseases for which there is no vaccine and no cure. If you think Samantha needs fresh air and exercise, train her to walk on a leash.

What to say and do If you feel you cannot keep Samantha indoors, attach a bell to her collar. This way she should make enough noise to warn the birds and mice of her presence. If she is not wearing a collar now, buy a breakaway collar—so she won't hang herself with it—and attach some identification in case she gets lost or hit by a car.

The protocol concerning gifts of small dead creatures is a question best answered by Miss Manners. Since the birds and mice are gifts, it would be rude to scold Samantha for bringing them to you. Treat Samantha as you would any friend who persists in bringing you inappropriate gifts—smile and thank her. If Samantha is sitting proudly by her catch when you arrive home from work, praise her. "Oh, what a good hunter, Samantha. Thank you for the nice mouse." Drop the mouse in the garbage when she isn't looking. The only way to keep Samantha from bringing live creatures into the house is to bolt the cat door when you aren't home.

Why this works Catching and bringing home small prey is as natural for a cat as is breathing. A noise-making device, such as a bell on her collar, may give prey enough warning to escape.

Preventative tips Keep your next cat strictly indoors except when you can give her direct supervision. An indoor cat won't irritate your bird-loving neighbors.

When you get a new kitten, plan to make it strictly an indoor cat. If the kitten never goes outside, it won't know it is missing anything and will live a long, comfortable, happy life in the safety of your home.

Biting, of children

I'm afraid we are going to have to get rid of our kitten, in spite of the fact that we all enjoy her very much. She is so cute and does so many amusing things that it is hard to think of parting with her. However, she scratches and bites my son when he plays with her. Is there any way to make her stop biting and scratching so we can keep her?

Why is my cat doing this? Kittens have no manners. They play roughly with their siblings, and they bite and scratch their mothers. This is all done in the spirit of great fun, but if you do not have thick skin or a layer of fur for protection, those little teeth can be very painful. Jimmy, at the age of three, is in the same developmental boat as Sassy. He has not yet learned that he can cause pain, and he may not be entirely clear on the concept that Sassy is a living creature, not one of his inanimate toys.

How can I make her stop? This is a two-step process. Jimmy must be taught that Sassy is a small living creature and that it hurts her when he hits her or squeezes her too tightly. Sassy must learn the difference between people and other cats and learn not to scratch or bite people.

What to say and do Watch Jimmy playing with Sassy so you will know where to start. If he is picking her up in a manner that is painful, squeezing her too tight, or not putting her down when she squirms, Sassy will bite him in self-defense. If Jimmy grabs a handful of Sassy's hair to pick her up, go immediately and place your hand under Sassy to support her weight and ease the pulling. Say, "Ouch, Jimmy. It hurts Sassy when you pick her up that way. Let me show you how to hold her nicely so she won't bite you."

Sit on the floor with Jimmy and Sassy and demonstrate the proper way to pick up a kitten. Place one hand under Sassy's rib cage and cradle her bottom with your other hand, lifting her off the floor.

Bring the hand under her rib cage across and next to your body, forming a cradle. Using the hand you have under her bottom, swing her hindquarters around so she is lying in the cradle. Now your other hand is free to stroke and scratch her. Jimmy may need a little practice, but he will soon catch on.

If Sassy is scratching or biting Jimmy because she wants to be put down and he is clutching her, tell him to put her down. Say, "Jimmy, Sassy has had all the love she can stand for right now. Put her down and let's go find your cars." Show Jimmy how to lower Sassy gently to the floor, and keep reminding him that she is not a toy and that it hurts Sassy to be squeezed or dropped, just as that treatment would hurt him.

If Sassy is biting Jimmy during play, teach Jimmy how to let Sassy know that she is hurting him and he wants her to stop. When Sassy plays too roughly, Jimmy should hold very still and say, "Ouch, Sassy, that hurts." Jimmy naturally has the high voice that kittens associate with the "stop" signal, and holding absolutely still lets Sassy know that the game is over for the moment.

The adults in the family should use the same technique for teaching Sassy not to play too roughly. The minute she starts to bite, even if her bites don't hurt you, keep perfectly still and squeal, "Ouch! That is too hard, Sassy. Don't bite." Use your highest, squeakiest voice.

Why this works Teaching Jimmy to respect other living creatures will eliminate Sassy's biting due to pain. Holding still and squeaking when Sassy bites mimics the behavior of her siblings. The kitten who has been doing the biting also pauses, thinks about it for a moment, and releases the victim.

Preventative tips Teach children the proper way to hold and pet kittens and always stop the activity if the child or the kitten starts playing too roughly.

Biting, of self

Our once beautiful cat just looks awful. He has chewed and scratched himself so much he has ugly sores all over his back and rump. He will be lying calmly in his favorite spot in the living room and he suddenly bolts upright and starts biting at himself. Why is he biting himself?

Why is my cat doing this? Take Kirby to the veterinarian right away. Kirby has a problem that is obviously causing him to itch terribly and he is biting at the area in an effort to make it stop. Like small children, cats do not understand that scratching or biting at a spot that itches gives only momentary relief. It will not eliminate the cause of the itch and damages the skin and invites infection to set in. The veterinarian can help you discover what is making Kirby itch.

How can I make him stop? You must find the underlying cause of his problem. There are many causes of itchy skin in cats, just as in people. Some cats have allergic reactions to fleas, and one flea bite will set off a reaction that causes the poor cat to itch all over. Some cats have allergies to food, pollens, grasses, cigarette smoke, wool, cat litter, or other substances and others suffer from stress-related (neurotic) itching. Ticks, mites, and fungus are a few more possibilities. Only an examination and possible testing by a veterinary specialist can determine the source of the itching and help you fix it. If your veterinarian is not able to determine the cause of Kirby's condition, he may recommend a veterinary dermatologist.

It is very important to take care of Kirby's problem immediately. Not only is he unsightly, he is awfully uncomfortable (remember how mosquito bites feel?), and his biting and scratching can cause sores on his body that, left untreated, can become infected and abscessed, causing Kirby to become very ill.

What to say and do Follow the advice of your veterinarian. The professional knows how best to deal with the cause of Kirby's problem and how to keep the problem from happening again. He can also tell you whether Kirby's condition is one that might be passed to other members of your household—other pets or children.

If Kirby has a flea allergy, be sure to ask the veterinarian how to eliminate fleas from your home and yard, and be sure to follow through on any treatment plan your specialist recommends. Too often, people stop treating their cat as soon as the sores start to heal and the hair starts growing back.

Why this works Removing what is irritating Kirby will stop his urge to bite at himself.

Preventative tips Check occasionally to make sure fleas haven't invaded your home. Look at the base of your cat's tail for the telltale black specks (flea dirt) that indicate the presence of fleas. Putting a drop of water on these specks will confirm the diagnosis— a reddish thread or ring will form as the water dissolves the specks.

Biting, when petted

Chrissy is a lovely cat, but sometimes she bites for no apparent reason. She will be lying on my lap getting petted and purring, and suddenly she turns and bites. She doesn't do this all the time, and she hasn't bitten either of us hard enough to break the skin, but it is hard enough to hurt. Is there something wrong with her?

Why is my cat doing this? Check Chrissy carefully to see if you can find a sore spot that causes her to bite you when you touch it. If you find a spot that is so tender Chrissy bites or protests when you touch it, take her to the veterinarian for treatment.

Is Chrissy spayed? Does she bite you only when she is in heat? Some female cats become excessively sensitive to petting while they are in heat, especially in the areas on the upper shoulders and neck and on the back, just above the tail. Unless you plan to breed Chrissy, have her spayed.

If Chrissy is spayed, she may just become overstimulated when she is being petted. Those same areas, across the upper shoulders and across the top of the rump, are where nerve bundles are concentrated. Some cats seem to have too little padding between their skin and these nerve bundles, and they bite to make the irritation stop. Some cats merely lay their teeth on your hand to tell you they have had enough; others can bite quite hard.

What to say and do If you do not plan to breed Chrissy, have her spayed. The hormone levels will drop off in a few weeks and the excessive sensitivity should disappear.

If Chrissy is spayed, pay attention to the circumstances leading up to her biting. If you can remember what happened just before she bit you, you can avoid future bites. If you notice that Chrissy bites when you are petting her in one of her sensitive areas, avoid petting her there. Are you stroking her back vigorously? Try petting with a little less enthusiasm. If you notice that she always bites after you have been petting her for five minutes or fifteen minutes, set a time limit on your petting and stop before she becomes too excited.

When Chrissy bites you, hold absolutely still, and in a high, squeaky voice say, "Ouch! That hurts, Chrissy." Keep your hand still. If she doesn't let go, again, in a high squeaky voice, say, "Ouch, Chrissy! Stop! That hurts!" When Chrissy lets go of your hand, put her on the floor and do not pet her for a while. Furnish her with a big stuffed toy so she can work off her pent-up desire to wrestle and bite.

Why this works Cats and kittens display the limits of their tolerance both physically and vocally. When one kitten is playing too roughly, its littermate will first bite and scratch. If the aggressor does not stop, the "victim" will squeal and stop playing. When one of the playmates squeals and becomes very still, it signals the other kitten that play has become too rough. When you say "Ouch" in a squeaky voice and stop moving your hand, Chrissy will know that she is hurting you and will stop.

Preventative tips Use the high, squeaky voice on kittens the first time they start playing too roughly with you. When siblings play too roughly, the victim squeals in pain and stops playing. This signals the aggressor that she is causing pain. Imitating the kitten's siblings is the quickest way to communicate with her.

Do not roughhouse with Chrissy with your bare hands. By playing roughly with her, you are telling her that her rough behavior is okay with you. Substitute a large stuffed toy for your hand. Hold the toy and rub her belly with it, and when she starts attacking the toy, let go and allow her to kick and bite it instead of your hand.

Bolting out the door

Blackie bolts out the door every time we open it. Even when he is sitting quietly on the other side of the room, apparently paying no attention, by the time the door is open wide enough for him to squeeze through, he has crossed the room and scooted outside. We want him to stay inside where he will be safe. How can we keep him from running out the door?

Why is my cat doing this? If Blackie is not neutered, have him neutered immediately! Blackie can detect a female in heat from at least three blocks away, and he will move heaven and earth to get to her. He will also likely spray urine all over the inside of your house in his attempts to notify females that he is available.

Blackie may have been allowed outdoors by his previous owners, or he may have been raised outside. He probably has not forgotten the adventure—new sights, new smells, and bugs, birds, and rodents to chase. Blackie just wants to go outside and play.

How can I make him stop? Make outside a shocking and undesirable place for Blackie. At the same time, make the indoors more interesting for him, so he will not be so interested in exploring the outside.

What to say and do Station a family member or friend outside the door with a metal pan and a big metal spoon. Put on your coat and say, "Good-bye, Blackie. See you later," just as you do when you are really leaving. Open the door, and when Blackie runs out, have your assistant bang on the pot with the spoon, stomp his feet, and yell. He can holler, "Oh, bad cat! Get back in the house," or "Yiii, yiii, yiii," while stamping and banging. The words aren't important—just as long as he makes a lot of noise.

Blackie will bolt back into the house like he has been shot! You quietly step outside and close the door. This needs to be repeated with all the doors to the house, and you may have to do it several times before Blackie becomes convinced that a big, noisy monster has moved into the neighborhood and decides to stay indoors, where it is safe. During the training period, which may last several days, be very careful not to let Blackie out. If he gets outside between sessions, it will be very difficult to convince him that the noise monster is always out there.

Make the inside of the house a fun place for Blackie. While cats like routine and do not like big changes in their environment, they do get bored with their toys. Blackie should have a variety of toys. Put some of them out of sight for a few days, then put away the toys he has been playing with and bring out the new ones. An upside-down cardboard box with entrance holes cut in the ends or paper bags with the tops folded over make great toys for cats. You can add interest to these toys by tossing a jingle ball inside or by making scratching noises on the back (where he can't see your hand) to entice him inside.

Why this works Cats do not like sudden, loud noises. They almost always will turn and run when they are startled. The yelling and pot-banging sound fearsome, and if Blackie is greeted with this shocking noise every time he tries to go out, he will quickly opt for the peace and quiet of indoor living.

Preventative tips Many cats live long, happy, healthy lives without ever going outdoors. Keep new pets strictly indoors. If they never go outside, they will not think they are missing something by staying inside, and there will be no possibility that they will be hit by a car.

Car, motion sickness in

We love to travel and have always taken our cat with us. Our old cat loved to travel and would run and get in her carrier any time we put it out.

Our new kitten is something else. She doesn't want to get in the carrier, and when we take her with us, she throws up before we have traveled the first mile. Is there some way we can make her stop throwing up so we can enjoy traveling with her?

Why is my cat doing this? There are two possible explanations for Oli's car sickness. She may have true motion sickness—the inability, or the undeveloped ability, to adjust to the motion of the vehicle—or she may be throwing up from fear. If Oli is one of those individuals whose inner ear will not adjust to motion, you may have to resign yourselves to traveling without her.

How can I make her stop? Break the problem into two parts. Oli's aversion to being in the carrier is one problem that may or may not have an effect on problem number two, the actual motion sickness. First, do everything you can to make Oli comfortable just being confined to her carrier. Even if her vomiting is brought on by the motion of the car, Oli will be a little less uncomfortable with the situation if she has learned to accept being in the carrier.

What to say and do Detailed instructions for overcoming carrier aversion are in the section Carrier, won't get in, but since Oli is not yet an adult with a strongly developed personality, you may be able to use the shorter version for kittens. Wash the carrier inside and out with mild soap and water and rinse thoroughly and dry. Place Oli's blanket and a favorite soft toy inside, or throw in a T-shirt you have worn to make the carrier smell like home. Pick a time of day when Oli is relaxed and spend a minute or two grooming or petting her, and offer her a taste of a treat such as strained baby food. Place a dab of the food in a small dish and place it just inside the door of her carrier. Place another dab on the dish, show it to her, and place it halfway back in the carrier. If she goes into the carrier to eat the treat, give her a second helping to reinforce the lesson, then quit before she gets too full. Repeat the lesson two or three times a day for the next few days until Oli is cheerfully getting into the carrier for her treat. Leave the carrier in the room for a few days so Oli sees it as just another piece of furniture, not something to fear.

Once Oli is over her fear of getting in the carrier, put her in the carrier and take her out to the car. Position the carrier facing frontward, rather than sideways, to allow Oli to position herself in the most comfortable direction. Get in the backseat with the carrier and give Oli her treat—the baby food. Repeat this session two or three times the first day. As soon as Oli calmly accepts being in the car and having her treat, drive one block, stop, give Oli her treat, and go home. Continue making longer trips until Oli is completely comfortable riding in the car.

If Oli is getting into the carrier without putting up a fuss, but is still getting carsick, it is time to see your veterinarian. Ask him whether medication will help Oli overcome her motion sickness. Do not attempt to give Oli any medication without your veterinarian's approval. Many human medications are poisonous to cats.

Why this works If Oli's motion sickness was indeed caused by her distress at being confined to the carrier, you have won the battle and she should no longer be getting carsick.

Preventative tips Introduce kittens to travel at a very young age so they won't be frightened.

See also:
Carrier, won't get in

Carrier, won't get in

know my cat should be in her carrier when we take her to the vet, but when we put her in her carrier she yells and claws at the door. Is there any way we can get her to go into the carrier without having a major battle?

Why is my cat doing this? Matilda probably associates being in the carrier with going to the veterinarian. Many cats are frightened by the unfamiliar, and the clinic is a strange place full of sounds, smells, people, and animals with which Matilda is not familiar. The carrier may also smell funny to Matilda. Matilda also senses that you are tense. She doesn't know that you are nervous because you dread the battle it takes to get her into the carrier, but she does sense that you are upset.

How can I make her stop? Matilda needs to be reintroduced to her carrier in a nonthreatening way. Reintroducing her to the carrier well in advance of your next trip to the veterinarian will allow you to be calm so Matilda won't sense your unease. Matilda might be less resistant to a cat bag or other soft carrier, and switching to one of these might easily eliminate the problem.

What to say and do Remove the bolts that hold the carrier together. Wash the carrier in mild soap and water and rinse it thoroughly to remove any possible odors.

Put the two separated halves of the carrier on the floor in the kitchen or living room and place Matilda's blanket in the bottom half. The sight and smell of her blanket may encourage her to walk into the carrier bottom for a nap. After a couple of days, place a small dish of Matilda's favorite treat in the carrier bottom. Baby food such as strained chicken or turkey is a good choice. Make whatever noise you normally use to tell Matilda you have a treat for her. In a cheerful voice say, "Matilda, I have a treat for you. Come and get it." Give her the treat in the carrier bottom several times a day for a few days.

While she is licking up the baby food, say, "See there, that's not so bad, is it?"

After a few days, set the top of the carrier on the bottom. Leave the door and bolts off for now. Prepare Matilda's treat and call her in the normal manner, saying, "Matilda, I have a treat for you." Allow Matilda to see and smell it, then place it in the back corner of the carrier. Continue to talk calmly and cheerfully to her. "See, Matilda, your treat is in here. Go in and get it." If she does not go into the carrier, take the top off and allow her to have her treat. Say, "Silly girl, this is the same place you always get your treat, it just had a lid on it. There really is nothing to be afraid of." Next time, place the lid on the bottom of the carrier, again show her the treat, and again place it in the back corner of the carrier. Say, "Look, Matilda, here's your treat. Go get it." Walk away and give her about fifteen minutes to make up her mind. If she refuses to go into the carrier for her treat, pick up the dish and put it in the refrigerator, saying, "Oh, I see you don't want a treat today." Try again several hours later. Make sure the treat is not becoming dried out and that it is at room temperature when you offer it.

Once Matilda accepts her treat in the carrier, put the door back on and bolt the two halves together. Leave the carrier out with the door open and continue offering her treats in it.

Next time you have to go to the veterinarian, keep the thought in mind that the doctor is a wonderful person, and the trip is for Matilda's benefit. Be relaxed and confident.

Why this works Matilda does not recognize her carrier when it is in pieces. By gradually reintroducing her, you remove the bad memories and replace them with good ones. Cats like small, confined areas, and often will rest and nap in their carriers if a familiar piece of bedding is provided for them.

Preventative tips Take your kitten, in her carrier, with you when you are running errands. Young kittens are very adaptable, and will quickly accept riding in their carrier once they see that no harm comes from these trips.

Chasing birds

We love birds and have several bird feeders in our yard, but if we can't find a way to make Wiggy leave them alone, we won't have them for long. Wiggy chases the birds when they land on the ground to pick up crumbs, and he climbs the trees and the feeders trying to get the birds. Is it possible to have a cat and still enjoy having birds in our yard, or are we going to have to choose between the two?

Why is my cat doing this? Wiggy has two reasons for chasing birds. The first is that even though he is well fed and he is probably reasonably sure you will feed him again tomorrow, a fellow can't be too careful, and "a bird in the hand . . ." This prey-catching instinct is what has made cats such valuable rodent exterminators over the centuries. It didn't take people long to discover that they could coax a cat to stay with them by feeding him tidbits, without fear that overfeeding would cause him to lose his interest in hunting. Perhaps someday cats will become domesticated enough to stop hunting for their food, but hundreds of years of living with humans have not eliminated their hunting instincts.

The other reason Wiggy is chasing the birds is because it is fun! Birds really are wonderful toys to cats. Their erratic movements and the fluttering noise of their wings are irresistible. That is why toys that mimic the look and behavior of birds are so successful with cats. This is one aspect of the cat's nature that humans have trouble accepting. Wiggy is not being cruel—he is just being a cat.

How can I make him stop? Don't expect Wiggy to stop being a cat. The best way to enjoy both your feathered friends and Wiggy is to keep Wiggy in the house. Veterinarians and other animal professionals agree that cats that are neutered or spayed, vaccinated, and kept indoors live longer, healthier lives. Far from depriving Wiggy of the pleasures of the great outdoors, you are protecting him from disease, cruelty from thoughtless or malicious humans, fights with other cats and dogs in the neighborhood, and automobiles.

What to say and do Help Wiggy adjust to life indoors by spending more time playing with him. A toy made from bird feathers or a piece of cloth tied to a string and attached to a stick will provide endless fun for the two of you. While you drag and twirl the bird, Wiggy can sharpen his stalking and pouncing technique and burn off some of his excess energy. These toys are available in pet stores, and playing with them will strengthen the bond between you and Wiggy.

If you don't want to make Wiggy an indoor cat, consider confining him to the house during the hours when the birds are feeding.

Why this works There is no sense in making yourself and Wiggy crazy trying to make him stop an activity that to him is as natural as breathing. Understanding Wiggy's nature will allow you to reach a compromise that will allow you to enjoy both your cat and your birds.

Preventative tips Many people keep both birds and cats inside their homes, and the two species live together in harmony and often become playmates. However, the cat-bird introduction usually happens when the kitten is very young—before it knows that it is a cat and that birds are its natural prey—and the birds in question are usually larger birds such as mynah birds and parrots, which are fully capable of teaching the cat to respect their strong, sharp beaks and claws.

Chewing, on electrical cords

Is there any way to make our kitten stop chewing on electrical cords? I have replaced the telephone cord twice because she chewed on it so much the telephone quit working. What can we do to make her stop before she cuts off our communications again?

Why is my cat doing this? This is a very dangerous behavior that you must correct immediately, before Sherry electrocutes herself, shorts out your wiring system, and burns down your house!

Electrical cord chewing is not an unusual activity for kittens. It is most likely a combination of their desire to chew on something because they are teething and the fact that the cord may resemble a small snake. The telephone cord is especially tempting to kittens because it moves, making it appear even more like prey. Generally, the cords to lamps, radios, and television sets remain stationary, but many people drag the telephone around the house while they are talking. This makes attacking and chewing on it even more delectable.

How can I make her stop? The way to make Sherry stop chewing is to cover the cords so she can't get to them, or to make them taste very bad. Playtime, involving toys that Sherry can stalk and pounce upon the way she attacks the telephone cord, will help, but this behavior is so dangerous that you must make her stop completely, not just slow down.

What to say and do Provide Sherry with a small, chewable toy to work on while she is teething and spend a little extra time playing with her by dragging or tossing toys she can chase and pounce on. If you don't want as much exercise as you get by dragging a toy around the room for her, use a kitty tease or other toy-on-a-string that you can flick or drag around for her to chase while you are sitting in a chair. But distraction and substitution are not enough to assure a quick end to this hazardous behavior. You must make the cords uninviting.

Out of sight, out of mind is a good rule for electrical cords, whether you are dealing with a toddler or a young animal. Gather up the excess cord behind your entertainment center and coil it into a small bundle. Tape or tie-wrap the bundle so it won't come unwound, then secure it against the back of the appliance with more tape. Cords, such as lamp cords, that must run across the floor should be taped down so Sherry can't get to them. Cords, such as the telephone cord, that can't be secured or taped down, should be treated with a bad-tasting substance, or wrapped in aluminum foil. Many cats hate the taste of Bitter Apple, a chewing repellent sold in pet stores. Joy dishwashing soap is also highly effective. Either of these substances can be applied to the telephone cord and any other cords that can't be secured or hidden from

Sherry. Wet a cloth with a generous amount of soap or Bitter Apple and rub it down the full length of the cord.

Use the *magazine toss*, *sharp clap*, or *hiss* if Sherry approaches an electrical cord. Say in a loud, sharp voice, "No, Sherry! Bad cat! Get away from the cord!" Be very aggressive in chasing her away from the cord. In extremely stubborn cases, wipe the cords with Tabasco sauce. This should be used as a last resort, because Tabasco is a very painful pepper preparation. However, it is not as painful as electrocution, and should be used if all else fails. Do, please, try Bitter Apple or Joy first.

Preventative tips Always start out the way you plan to continue. Don't let Sherry get away with dangerous or destructive behavior even once, no matter how cute she looks. It is very easy to train cats to perform an act that brings them some reward (she caught the prey and the chewing relieved her teething pains), but it is difficult and time consuming to train them to stop the behavior.

Chewing, on fingers

Our big brown tabby is almost a perfect cat. He doesn't have any bad habits except he likes to chew on my fingers when we get in bed. He doesn't bite hard enough to break the skin, but my fingers are raw and sore. I have been getting up and putting him out of the room so I can sleep, but I miss his company. Why can't he just curl up and go to sleep like a normal cat?

Why is my cat doing this? Some feline behaviorists believe that the chewing or gnawing cats do is a carryover from kittenhood. The kitten derived comfort from nursing and translated it into chewing as he grew. Others believe that this is a habit formed during the kitten's teething stage, when chewing gives some relief to sore gums.

How can I make him stop? At a full year old, Bear is finished teething, but you should check his mouth to make sure he is not chewing to relieve soreness. If you see anything suspicious, such as red or swollen gums, have your veterinarian examine Bear and correct the problem.

If Bear is not chewing to relieve a sore mouth, his chewing is most likely just a bad habit and one that can be broken, but you will have to be firm and consistent. Bear might be willing to accept a substitute for his chewing, such as a small, chewable toy or stick. Be sure not to offer him something that could splinter and injure his mouth or stomach.

The other thing you must do is make your fingers taste bad. There are many substances that cats do not enjoy tasting. Tabasco sauce and liquid soap are among the most effective, but should only be used if you have exceptionally tough skin, since both substances can cause skin irritation. Care must be also be taken not to rub your eyes or put your fingers into your own mouth after they have been coated with Tabasco or soap. Most cats are repelled by the taste and smell of citrus fruits. Rubbing orange or lemon peel or oil of peppermint (not peppermint extract) on your fingers at bedtime will make them unappetizing to Bear. Again, don't rub your eyes or mouth, as citrus peel may cause irritation to your eyes and mucous membranes. There are also commercial preparations that taste bad to cats, such as Bitter Apple, which is sold at pet stores. Read the label carefully before you apply any product to your skin.

You need to communicate to Bear that his chewing is not pleasurable for you. This will reinforce the bad taste he gets from biting into your coated fingers. When Bear puts his mouth on your fingers, say, "Ouch, Bear, stop. That hurts," and push his head away. When he again attempts to chew your fingers, push his head away again, saying, "No, Bear. Don't chew on me. That hurts." Continue to push him away and complain. If he won't stop, and you are tired of pushing him away, put him out of the room. Carry him to the door and put him out. Say, "I'm sorry, Bear, but it hurts when you chew on me. You can't sleep with me if you insist on chewing on my fingers."

If you are not too softhearted, tapping Bear on the nose when he tries to chew your fingers will work faster than pushing him away. Using one finger, gently tap Bear's nose every time he starts to take your finger in his mouth. Say firmly, "No, Bear. No chewing."

You must be consistent and scold Bear and either push him away or tap him on the nose every time he starts to chew.

Why this works The consistent use of a bad-tasting substance will soon convince Bear that your fingers no longer taste good, and he will stop chewing for that reason.

Scolding, pushing away, and tapping on the nose are the methods mother cats use to discourage their kittens from pestering them. Bear understands this form of discipline.

Preventative tips Never let your kitten bite or scratch you. Stop playing immediately when he bites, and push him away or leave the area yourself.

Claws, accidental scratching and snagging

My cat is driving me crazy. She sits on my lap and kneads, and her claws feel like needles. Sometimes she pats or rubs her paws on my face and arms and leaves small scratches. She isn't mad when she does this, but her claws grow extra long and stick out all the time—I don't think she knows she is hurting me. Her extra-long claws also snag in my clothing and the furniture. She uses her scratching post and doesn't scratch the furniture. I don't want to have her declawed, but I don't know what else to do.

Why is my cat doing this? Sapphire does indeed love you. When she sits on your lap and purrs and kneads, she is displaying the kind of contentment she enjoyed as a tiny kitten, when she was nursing. Nursing kittens knead their mother's stomach to stimulate the flow of milk. Although Sapphire's expression of bliss may be

painful, rest assured that she is exhibiting her love and has no inten-
tion of hurting you. The love pats that result in minor scratches are
truly accidental.

Because Sapphire's claws are a little longer than normal, they
don't retract fully. What would be a soft, very enjoyable love pat is
painful because Sapphire's claws extend beyond the end of her paws.
The extra length of Sapphire's claws is also the cause of the snagging
of clothing and furniture.

Having her claws catch in the furniture and carpeting is probably
as annoying to her as it is to you. You can imagine how frustrating it
would be to have your foot stick to the floor every few steps. Sapphire
can't take a graceful walk across the room without snagging herself
and having to stop and disengage the offending claw. Even if her
claws were not extra long, Sapphire would still cause you pain when
she sat on your lap kneading away. There is no way to train Sapphire
not to knead, but you can make it less painful.

How can I make her stop? Sapphire just needs a manicure,
not to be declawed. Declawing is relatively expensive elective surgery
(a procedure that does not improve the quality of the cat's life). It is
painful, and every surgery carries some elements of risk to the patient.
Declawing should be done only if the situation has become so unbear-
able that otherwise Sapphire would have to be put to sleep.

After her manicure, Sapphire's shorter, blunter claws will not
cause you any pain when she kneads your knees, and her love pats
will be soft and sweet, as she intends them to be. Trimming off the
sharp points and extra length from her claws will also relieve Sapphire of the aggravation of constantly getting her claws caught in the
rug, clothing, and upholstery, and save wear and tear on those items.

Sapphire will need her manicure repeated at about two-week in-
tervals to keep her claws short and blunt. An alternative to semi-
monthly manicures is to have your veterinarian equip Sapphire with
vinyl nail protectors. These are applied somewhat like women's false
fingernails and provide a soft cushion between the cat's claws and
your possessions and tender skin. Vinyl nail protectors require professional application, so the product is sold only through your veterinarian.

There is another product that uses small beads to cover the tips of the cat's claws. The nail tip is covered with a special adhesive that comes in the kit, and then is slipped into the hole in the bead. The beads make an interesting clicking sound when the cat walks.

Both the vinyl nail protectors and the beads will be lost as the claws are shed and must be periodically replaced.

Why this works Periodic clipping, or covering the claws with soft vinyl or beads, removes or covers the needle-sharp tips of your cat's claws. The blunter, clipped or covered claw will not scratch you or catch in clothing or upholstery and carpeting.

Preventative tips Start clipping kittens' claws when they are young so they will learn to tolerate periodic trimming.

Climbing, on drapes

Our three-month-old kitten is ruining our drapes. He climbs up them several times a day and either snags them or pulls the hooks off the rod. Sometimes he climbs up and just hangs by his nails, pulling little holes in the fabric. We can't afford to buy new drapes every few months, and we want to keep the kitten. How can we make him stop climbing the drapes?

Why is my cat doing this? Skippy has a number of reasons for climbing the drapes. Cats love to be in high places. From the top of the drapes, Skippy can survey his territory to see if any prey is available, while remaining safely out of the reach of predators that might be looking for him. While we hope our homes are free of mice and other critters that might be of interest to Skippy, cats are eternal optimists, and never pass up an opportunity to scout the terrain. We also hope that we have no coyotes or other predators in our homes, but cats retain enough of their wild heritage to remain cautious and seek out high places. Skippy also has an excess of energy, and climbing the drapes is a natural way for him to expend this energy—and while he's at it, he can practice his climbing techniques, just in case an unfriendly dog or coyote happens to come in someday. Skippy knows that if he is chased by a large predator, the safest thing he can do is climb a tree.

How can I make him stop? One solution is to move the drapes out of Skippy's reach. Consider using balloon drapes that decorate the window but remain well out of reach of even the most determined curtain climber. The lazy man's solution to curtain climbing is to tie a big, loose knot in the drapes, raising them off the floor out of Skippy's reach. However, if you want your home to look like a home, you can train Skippy to leave the drapes alone.

What to say and do Provide Skippy with the high places he craves. There are some beautiful tall scratching posts made especially for cats to climb. These have resting shelves or baskets, and cats love to scamper to the top and survey their territory, then settle down for a nap. A less expensive climbing alternative is a simple wooden stepladder. Two stepladders with plank bridges provide an interesting indoor tree where Skippy can climb, play, and nap.

Skippy also needs some help burning off his excess energy. The easiest way to do this is to get another kitten of the same age as a playmate. If this isn't practical, play with Skippy by tossing a ball—Ping-Pong, foam, or fabric—for him to chase, or drag a kitty tease toy or a string with a light toy, piece of cloth, or paper tied to it. Place a row of *shaker cans* on the curtain rod to discourage Skippy when you aren't around to supervise him. When he starts to run up the draperies, the shaker cans will fall and frighten him away.

When Skippy tries climbing the drapes while you are in the room, pluck him off the drapes and carry him to his approved climbing place. Say, "No, Skippy, the drapes aren't for climbing. Use your nice ladder." If Skippy doesn't get the message after being relocated a few times, use the *magazine toss* and *hand clap* to let him know his behavior is not acceptable. Say sharply, "No, Skippy! Get off the drapes!" Be consistent. Don't allow him to climb the drapes one time and scold him the next. Correct him every time he does it and he'll soon catch on.

Why this works Providing Skippy with a high vantage point satisfies his need to be "above it all." Consistent correction when he climbs forbidden items convinces him that his own perch is better.

Preventative tips Provide interesting places for the kitten to climb and high places for him to perch on before you bring him home. Correct the kitten the first time he climbs the curtains, no matter how cute he is.

Climbing, on people

We just adore our kitten, except for one bad habit. When he wants some attention or thinks we have food he climbs up our legs. Not only does he leave painful scratches on our legs, he has ruined many pairs of stockings and has snagged our clothes. How can we make him stop using us for climbing posts?

Why is my cat doing this? Theodore is behaving like a normal kitten, and kittens have no manners. It is perfectly natural for him to be fairly outspoken about what he wants. If he can't reach it, he will jump or climb in his efforts to attain his goals. He doesn't realize that he is causing you pain or damaging your clothing.

How can I make him stop? This training should have been done before the kitten came to your home. Leg climbing usually begins somewhere between four and eight weeks, depending on the individual kitten's nature. Although kittens from accidental litters—that is, from people who allow their unneutered pets to have unplanned litters—go to new homes at the age of six weeks or less, most breeders do not allow their kittens to go to new homes until they are ten to twelve weeks of age. During the period between six and twelve weeks, the kittens have their first two vaccinations and continue to learn self-grooming techniques from their mothers and human manners from the breeder's family. But it is certainly not too late to correct this painful and destructive behavior. The retraining is fairly simple and can be done even if both your hands are full.

What to say and do Wear jeans around the house until your kitten is trained to stay off your legs. Don't panic; this is only going to take a day or two. Clip the kitten's claws; it is only necessary to clip the little needle points off so he won't draw blood during the brief training period.

When the kitten starts to climb your jeans-clad leg, just stomp your foot. Leave the ball of your foot on the floor and jiggle your heel up and down until the kitten falls off.

Say in a harsh voice, "Ouch, you little devil, that hurts! Get off! Get off my leg! Don't climb my legs, that hurts," and jiggle your leg until he falls off. If your hands are free and there is a lightweight magazine or an empty manila file folder available, pick up the magazine or folder and lightly swat him (gently; you just want to startle him, not hurt or punish him) while saying again, in a sharp voice, "Ouch! That doesn't feel good! Your little claws are sharp! Get off!" You can also dislodge him by plucking him off your leg and setting him on the floor when he climbs. Be sure to lift upward to disengage his claws.

Swatting is done with an extremely light touch. The combination of the rush of air caused by the magazine or file folder, the light pat, the noise of the magazine, and your harsh voice is enough. Don't hit hard enough to hurt. Try a few practice swats at your own leg or arm to see how little force is necessary to startle the kitten without causing him any other discomfort.

Why this works The short drop from your knee to the floor isn't enough to hurt the kitten, but the combination of being jiggled or swatted off your leg, the noise of the magazine, and your harsh, disapproving voice makes leg climbing an unpleasant experience. Kittens only do things that they find pleasant or otherwise rewarding (such as getting a few loving caresses or something good to eat).

Preventative tips Correct unwanted behavior the first time and every time it happens. Remember, what is cute behavior in a kitten may be completely unacceptable in a fully grown cat.

See also:
Appendix (Clipping Claws)

Defecating, far from litter box

Our three-year-old cat has just recently started defecating under the dining room table. She has always used the litter box in the past. We don't understand why she is doing this, and she is ruining the carpet. How can we make her go back to using her litter box?

Why is my cat doing this? Cats hide their feces to prevent predators from locating them. They prefer soft, dry, loose soil or commercial cat litter because it is easy to dig in. Because of this, if a litter box is provided cats will use it, usually without any training on the part of the owner.

When cats urinate or defecate in an unusual place, it is a signal that something is out of whack in their world. The fact that Nikki is defecating at a distance from the litter box indicates there may be a disturbance in its vicinity.

How can I make her stop? Since Nikki has always used her litter box in the past, you will have to do a little detective work to learn why she stopped. First, take Nikki to your veterinarian to make sure there is nothing physically wrong with her, such as a digestive upset or an infestation of roundworms or tapeworms.

Try to determine whether anything changed in the house to cause Nikki to avoid her litter box. Has the litter box been moved to an unacceptable location? Nikki's litter box needs to be in a relatively quite spot, away from the heavy traffic pattern. Is it possible that

Nikki was accidentally locked out of the room where her litter box is located? Cats will try very hard to confine their elimination to the litter box, but if they can't get to it in a reasonable time, they will take the next available spot. New household members can also upset the cat and make her seek another place to defecate. An inquisitive dog, a rambunctious child, or an adult who walks too fast or too heavily past the litter box may make Nikki feel that her box is not in a safe location. A newly installed telephone or doorbell would also be likely to frighten Nikki away from her box. Like people, cats like a little privacy and peace and quiet while they are using the toilet.

What to say and do Do not scold or punish her—Nikki isn't using the carpet as a toilet because she wants to, but because something is wrong. Never, never rub Nikki's nose in the spot—she will not understand why you are doing it. She will be frightened and confused and may become afraid of you.

Thoroughly clean the spot under the table and treat it with an odor-eliminating product (such as Outright, available from your veterinary or from pet stores) designed especially for pet odors. Cover the area with heavy plastic or aluminum foil to discourage Nikki from returning to that spot. If you see her scratching around the area, pick her up and gently carry her to her litter box. Say in a calm voice, "Oh, no, Nikki, that's not where we go to the bathroom. You want to use your nice litter box."

Make sure other household members are not annoying Nikki when she tries to use her litter box. If you have visiting children or loud adults, Nikki might be pleased to have her litter box moved to a quiet part of the house until they leave. Make sure you show Nikki where you put her litter box, so she can find it when she needs it. If the child, loud adult, or new dog is to be a permanent addition to the household, find a new, quieter location for Nikki's litter box. Try adding a screen to enclose the box on three sides and give Nikki some privacy.

Why this works Cats are naturally fastidious creatures. Given their choice, they will always use a clean litter box that is placed in a quiet, convenient location.

Preventative tips Place litter boxes in quiet, low-traffic areas where there is some privacy for the cat. Make sure that the location is such that Nikki can't accidentally be closed out of the room where her box is located. Train children and dogs to respect the cat's right to privacy.

Defecating, in houseplants

Our new kitten has chosen the potted plants as his litter box. He makes a terrible mess, scattering dirt from the pot all over the carpet, and, of course, the plants smell bad.

Why is my cat doing this? Often, cats and kittens avoid their litter boxes in an effort to signal their people that they have a medical problem. Have your veterinarian examine Jenks to make sure he is in good health. Also, make sure Jenks has the privacy he needs to use his litter box. It should be kept clean and placed out of the traffic area and in a location where small children and the dog can't annoy him.

It is possible that your kitten was raised out of doors and is accustomed to going to the bathroom in dirt. The filler in your litter box may smell and feel strange to him. However, cats like to scratch in loose or soft surfaces, and the dirt in the planters may just be another attractive place to scratch. He may also be avoiding his litter box because it is not clean enough to suit him.

How can I make him stop? You have to discover why Jenks isn't using his litter box. Make sure Jenks has a clean litter box in a quiet location where he can feel safe. If Jenks is choosing the dirt in the potted plants over his litter box, you will have to help him learn to prefer his litter box. If his litter box isn't clean, he may be using the potting soil because his own toilet smells too awful.

What to say and do Because cats like a nice, dry place to dig, keeping the soil damp in the planters will discourage him. If Jenks is so bold that he will use the planters for his litter box while you are in the room, pick him up and carry him to his litter box. Say, "No, Jenks! That is not your litter box. Here is your own nice clean litter box. This is where good kitties go to the bathroom." Be gentle. You don't want to punish Jenks or make him afraid of you; you just want to retrain him. When you are too far away to pick Jenks up before he gets into the planter, use the *magazine toss* and *hand clap.* Say, "No, Jenks! Get out of there!"

If Jenks is not using his litter box at all, mix potting soil or yard dirt into the litter. Start with half plain dirt and gradually increase the amount of litter until Jenks is using plain litter with no dirt added.

At the same time, make the plants unattractive for Jenks to use as a litter box. Place pieces of screen or a layer of decorative rock or broken hazelnut shells on top of the dirt. These materials make it difficult for Jenks to get to the dirt and are especially helpful if you can't supervise Jenks every minute.

Spraying the pot and soil with a commercial cat repellent will encourage Jenks to find another rest room. Read the container labels carefully to make sure the repellent is safe to use indoors. If possible smell it in advance of purchasing it, so you don't buy a product that is better at repelling people than pets. Citrus peel placed in the planters will discourage Jenks, but the scent will last only for a few days. Fresh peelings will have to be placed in the pot a couple times a week.

In addition to discouraging Jenks with unpleasant scents, use the *shaker can.* Place several shaker cans around the rims of the pots. When Jenks tries to jump into a potted plant, he will dislodge the noisy shaker can and be frightened away from the plant.

Why this works Cats prefer clean, soft, loose soil, sand, or similar material for their toilet. Providing a clean, fresh litter box, combined with making the planters unattractive to him, will convince your cat that the litter box is a better toilet than the planters.

Preventative tips New kittens and cats should be confined to a small room, such as the bathroom, for the first few hours. This period will allow you to make sure the litter box is being used. Once the kitten has used the litter box in his new home, the door should be left open so he can explore on his own. Kittens can always find their way back to the litter box if they are allowed to walk out of the room, rather than being carried.

See also:
Appendix (Litter-Box Care)

Defecating, near litter box

Our cat has always used his litter box, but recently he has started defecating right next to it instead of in it. Why has he suddenly decided not to use his litter box?

Why is my cat doing this? Sebastian is trying to tell you something is wrong. Most cats don't even have to be trained to use the litter box. The soft, loose, dry litter is the ideal place for them to bury their stool and urine so predators won't know there is a cat in the vicinity.

The smooth, hard surface of the linoleum-covered floor is not a place Sebastian would normally choose for his toilet. By remaining close to the box, Sebastian is signaling that he wants to use his litter box, but is prevented from doing so because something is wrong with the box or he is having some physical difficulty.

How can I make him stop? First you must determine the cause of the problem. This will take a little detective work on your part. Once you have found the cause of Sebastian's displeasure, you can easily remedy the situation.

What to say and do Have your veterinarian examine Sebastian to see if he has a physical problem. Digestive difficulties resulting in loose stools or hard stools may be causing Sebastian to have gas pains or painful elimination. Since this pain happens while he is in the litter box, he may be looking for a place where he can move his bowels without pain. Roundworms or tapeworms or other internal parasites can produce enough physical discomfort to cause them to avoid their litter box. While these parasites are easily eliminated, the treatment is different in each case. Your veterinarian can best determine whether Sebastian has internal parasites and prescribe the best course of treatment.

Sebastian may also be telling you that the litter box needs your attention. The litter box should be kept scrupulously clean. Solids should be scooped out at least once a day, and the litter should be changed completely when one third of it is wet, or every week at a minimum. Dump the used litter into a plastic bag, tie the top, and place it in the garbage. Scrub the box with soap and hot water and rinse thoroughly. Pour about one tablespoon of bleach into the box, add water, and swish it around, then rinse thoroughly once more. This will kill any lingering odor-causing bacteria. Dry and refill the box with fresh litter and put it back in its usual spot. There are litter deodorants that some cats find extremely objectionable. If you have recently changed brands of litter, go back to the old brand for a day or two. Gradually mix in larger and larger amounts of the new litter until Sebastian becomes used to the new texture and scent. Be aware that you may have to abandon the new litter if Sebastian is repelled by its odor. It may give him a headache or upset his stomach, in the same way people are affected by various perfumes.

Sebastian may have decided that he would prefer not to defecate in the same box where he urinates. In multicat households it is not at all uncommon to observe that the cats urinate in one litter box and defecate in another. Try providing Sebastian with a second box and see if that makes him happy. If you have recently added another cat to your household, by all means provide a second litter box. The cats may decide to have "yours" and "mine" litter boxes, or both may urinate in one box and defecate in another.

An inch or two of litter is usually enough to put in the litter box, but try filling the box a little deeper to see if Sebastian just wants to be able to dig deeper.

Why this works Cats appear to instinctively choose to use the litter box. Quickly determining the cause of the problem and eliminating it will get the cat back in the litter box before bad habits can develop.

Preventative tips Keep litter boxes clean, easily available, and away from traffic. Seek veterinary assistance at the first sign of change in litter-box habits.

Depression

My cat has been so droopy lately. I didn't think cats could get depressed, but she isn't eating or playing or keeping her fur looking as nice as she used to, and I'm getting worried about her. What can I do to make her stop lying around like a lump and go back to being her cheerful, well-groomed self?

Why is my cat doing this? Certainly cats can get depressed or have their feelings hurt. They appear to have a whole range of emotions. A little thought on your part might come up with the answer to Marguerite's less than perky demeanor. If you can't quickly come up with a reason for her depression, such as the loss of a loved person or animal companion, take her to your veterinarian for a thorough examination. Depression in cats is sometimes the only sign they give their owners that they are in need of medical attention. Marguerite has no way to communicate to you that she has a headache or a stomachache or an abscessed tooth. All she can do is curl up in misery and wait for you to find the cause of her problem. There is a wide variety of feline ailments for which depression or lethargy is one of the symptoms. Cats who have been fastidious groomers in the past don't neglect their fur unless they are indeed ill or distressed.

How can I make her stop? Having ruled out medical problems, think hard about what has changed in Marguerite's small world. If she has lost a person or another pet, it is normal for her to be subdued for a short period, but life does go on, and after a reasonable amount of mourning, it is time to get back into her routine. Even changes that seem insignificant to you may be enough to throw Marguerite into a tailspin.

What to say and do Try to reverse the change you think might be causing Marguerite's depression. Did you switch brands or types of cat litter? Maybe the deodorant in the new brand gives her a headache—or maybe the new clumping litter clings to her feet, or maybe the clay litter feels sharp to her. If you have changed litter, go back to the old one for a while or try a completely different litter, such as shredded paper towels.

If you have moved Marguerite's litter box to a new location, consider putting it back where it was and moving it toward the desired new location a few inches at a time so she has a chance to get used to the idea.

Heaven help you if you threw out her favorite toy. Did she have a straggly, dirty, soggy mouse she was always dragging around with her? Did you finally get so embarrassed that you threw it away? Did you finally take that shredded scratching post to the dump? Uh-oh! Rub some catnip on that new scratching post and rub her paws on it (gently, cheerfully) to place her scent on it. An interactive toy such as a kitty tease or feathers tied to a small stick with a length of string are surefire winners at getting the attention of the most jaded cat. Spending time playing with her might earn her forgiveness.

Has she been locked out of her usual sleeping spot? Perhaps the new puppy is now sleeping in the utility room where Marguerite has always had her bed, or the youngster she used to cuddle with has decided, now that he or she is a young adult, more privacy is needed. Teenagers have a lot on their minds, and the sweet little girl who used to go get Marguerite at bedtime may now be focused on other things. She may not be aware that Marguerite is wondering why she has been abandoned. Make sure Marguerite is getting plenty of attention and affection, and if your teenager is not feeling too grown up to sleep with the cat, remind her to take Marguerite into her room before she closes the door for the night.

Why this works Exercise, for cats and humans alike, gets the blood circulating and provides the energy to take a new interest in life. Attention also works the same for both people and cats. We all feel better if someone will give us a little of their undivided attention.

Preventative tips Try to remember Marguerite's needs when you are making changes in the household. You might feel silly about explaining proposed changes to your cat, but such discussions seems to help cats accept changes. Marguerite will appreciate the attention even if she doesn't understand your words.

See also:
Meowing, constant

Digging in flower beds

My cat has been using my flower beds as his litter box. He has dug up or buried a number of small plants and has rolled on others and crushed them. It is very unpleasant when I accidentally unearth one of his deposits. How can I make him stop digging in the flower beds?

Why is my cat doing this? Jasper is most likely looking for a clean rest room. Cats have survived for thousands of years by being very careful not to announce their presence until they know it is safe to do so. Part of this caution includes carefully burying their urine and feces so predators cannot smell it. Cats love to dig in soft, loose soil, which is what makes it so easy to train them to use a litter box indoors—the litter allows them to dig easily to the desired depth and allows plenty of material for carefully covering the deposit. Your lovingly prepared flower bed makes an ideal litter box for Jasper. Your tender seedlings are simply in the way of Jasper's excavations and are accidentally dislodged while he is going about his business.

Jasper's rolling may have two causes. He may simply be expressing his enjoyment of his wonderful life, or you may have planted something that Jasper finds particularly appealing—so appealing, in fact, that he wants to rub the scent all over his body.

How can I make him stop? The simplest way to end Jasper's demolition of the flower beds is to keep him strictly indoors. That will immediately end the problem of his fertilizing your garden and destroying your seedlings. Your veterinarian will agree that Jasper will live a longer, healthier life if you will make him an indoor-only cat. If you want Jasper to continue to enjoy the outdoors, consider allowing him out only under direct supervision. If you are with Jasper, you can shoo him out of the flower beds. Be sure to provide him with a clean litter box indoors.

What to say and do Cats are very difficult to control outdoors. Many cats who are underfoot in the house will run from their owners when they are outdoors. It may be possible to train Jasper to accept wearing a harness and leash. This will give you complete control and will prevent him jumping the fence to practice his mischief on the neighbor's flower beds.

If possible, place a clean litter box in the garage and provide Jasper access to it. When Jasper starts digging in the flower bed, pick him up and carry him to the litter box. In a horrified voice say, "No, no, Jasper. That's not your toilet. Here. Use your nice clean litter box." This, of course, is much easier to control if Jasper is on a leash.

If you want to let Jasper continue to roam freely outdoors, provide him with a breakaway collar (which will allow him to escape if it gets snagged on something) and identification so you can be located if he becomes lost. Keep the soil in your flower beds wet—Jasper will prefer his nice dry litter box.

There are several commercial cat repellents available in nursery and garden departments and in pet stores. You can also use a more organic approach to keeping Jasper out of the flower beds; cayenne pepper and citrus peel (orange and lemon) are repellent to cats. If you have a small garden or lots of citrus peelings you can simply scatter peelings on the ground to keep Jasper out. However, natural substances quickly lose their effectiveness and must be replaced often. Mulching with ponderosa pinecones or broken hazelnut shells is an attractive way to keep Jasper and other neighborhood cats and dogs out of your garden.

Look to see whether Jasper has done his rolling on any particular plant. If he has, ask at the nursery you patronize whether that plant is particularly appealing to cats. You may want to choose a replacement Jasper won't enjoy quite so enthusiastically.

Why this works Cats will instinctively avoid unpleasant odors or materials such as broken nut shells that are uncomfortable on their feet.

Preventative tips Keep all your cats indoors. They will live longer, healthier lives—and so will your plants.

Drooling

Molly is a lovely cat, but her drooling is disgusting. How can I make her stop?

Why is my cat doing this? Cats drool for many reasons. Some cats drool when they are scared. If Molly drools all the time, she may have a serious medical problem. Have your veterinarian examine Molly to make sure she doesn't have a decayed or broken tooth, an abscess, or some other sore spot in her mouth. Molly may be afraid to close her mouth because of a painful condition, and her open mouth allows the saliva to escape. Drooling may also be a symptom of other medical conditions. If this is the case, your veterinarian can find the cause of her problem and help you eliminate it.

Drooling because of excess saliva production is something Molly can't control. She does not have lips to help her contain the excess saliva she is producing because what you are cooking for dinner smells wonderful and she knows she is going to get some, or because she is so thrilled with being petted. Many cats knead and drool during petting.

How can I make her stop? Like Pavlov's dogs, Molly has learned that she will get something good as soon as you finish your meal preparation and she is drooling in anticipation. This is a learned response that can be unlearned. You have to teach Molly that she will not be given a reward for drooling on your feet while you are cooking.

What to say and do If Molly is drooling in response to cooking odors, feed her a regular evening meal before you start dinner and stop giving her a taste of your dinner. Put Molly out of the room while you prepare and eat your dinner. After a week or two of not getting a treat at the end of your cooking session, Molly will stop drooling while you are cooking. I know this is difficult. Humans equate food with love, and it is natural to want to share the good things in life with Molly.

If you really can't bear to deny Molly special treats from the table, save a little of your dinner and give it to her the following evening before you start preparing that evening's meal. You can even go so far as to warm Molly's treat in the microwave so it is truly special. Do take care to test the temperature of the treat before you give it to Molly—it is easy to get things too hot for the cat when using the microwave to warm them.

If Molly is drooling because she loves you so much and adores being petted by you, there is not much you can do to correct the situation, but you can make it a little easier to deal with your slobberpuss. Get the Kleenex box and a hand towel before you sit down for your evening of television and cuddles. Spread the towel over your lap to catch any occasional drips. When Molly starts kneading and slobbering, just get a tissue and wipe her chin. When the petting session is over, drop the used tissue in the wastebasket and put the towel in the laundry hamper.

Why this works Pavlov's dogs were trained to drool in anticipation of food. Cooking food, but not giving any to your cat, is the reverse of Pavlov's method. It takes longer than training because there is no reward, but eventually your cat will stop drooling when you cook because she will learn not to expect a treat.

Preventative tips Don't train Molly to expect some of what you are having for dinner. It is all right to give cats treats as long as the treat is small enough not to interfere with their normal diet (a teaspoonful is a good-sized treat for a cat). But care must be taken not to teach Molly that you are cooking for her pleasure. Schedule Molly's treats so they don't coincide with your mealtimes.

Eating, off kitchen counter

My cat steals food from the kitchen counter. If I leave a roast or a chicken out to thaw, I come home from work and find the cat has dragged it into the living room, torn open the wrapper, and eaten some or all of it. I have to clean up the mess and then find something else for dinner. She is well fed and doesn't need to steal food. How can I make her stop?

Why is my cat doing this? Cats like variety in their diet, and Prissy is just helping herself to something that tastes good. She may also be enjoying the adventure of capturing her own dinner—that is, getting for herself a meal that wasn't placed in her dish.

How can I make her stop? You could make an extended, vigorous, determined effort to train Prissy to leave your thawing dinner alone. If you are willing to make this goal the focus of your life for the next six weeks or so, you might even succeed. However, attempts to make Prissy stop helping herself to something that tastes as wonderful as "captured" raw roast of beef or chicken breast will more likely end in nervous breakdowns for both of you.

Professional animal trainers use rewards of good-tasting food to get quick results in teaching animals to do things they normally would not do. The trainers of the animals used in the filming of *Homeward Bound: The Incredible Journey* trained the Himalayan cats to perform such unnatural stunts as "hugging" the dogs, swimming, and riding on a floating log by giving them food rewards. Thoroughly trained animals will continue to perform their stunt long after the trainer has ceased reinforcing the training with food rewards.

Prissy has no reluctance to jump up on the counter, since cats do that all the time without any reward at all. Often, when she jumps on the counter she also finds a food reward waiting for her. She has doubly trained herself to do something she enjoys—jump up on something and get the reward of your thawing meal.

What to say and do In the interest of preserving your sanity and your otherwise good relationship with Prissy, thaw the meat somewhere other than the kitchen counter. Try placing the roast or chicken in the refrigerator in the evening, before you go to bed. If the meat hasn't completely thawed by dinnertime the following evening, it can be hurried along by placing it, still in its wrapper, in a bowl of cold water, or by using the defrost cycle on your microwave. If you prefer to defrost your entrée at room temperature, hide it from Prissy by placing it in the oven or microwave. Nutritionists (and the U.S. Department of Agriculture) say, however, that thawing foods outside the refrigerator vastly increases the risk of food poisoning, and people are strongly urged not to do it.

You can attempt to retrain Prissy to stay off the counter by using many *shaker cans*, turned on their sides so they roll easily, and covered with newspaper so she can't see to avoid them. You can also cover the countertop with sopping wet bath towels or with strips of double-faced masking tape.

Why this works Shaker cans will make a lot of unpleasant noise, and wet towels and double-faced tape are most distasteful underfoot. The discomfort Prissy experiences with the shaker cans, wet towels, or tape may outweigh the possibility of finding a juicy thawing steak.

Preventative tips Keep tempting food stored in places where Prissy can't get at them when you are not there to supervise her activities.

Eating, off the table

Our cat is making mealtime miserable. He jumps right up in the middle of the table and tries to help himself to our dinner. We have to shut him in the bathroom when we have company so he won't embarrass us in front of our guests. We hate having to explain to guests why Clancy is locked in the bathroom, but that is better than having him on the table. What can we do to make him behave?

Why is my cat doing this? Mealtime is probably a time when your family gets together and shares news of the day and plans for the future. Part of the attraction your dinner table holds for Clancy is his desire to join in the exchange. There is also the attraction of the delicious smells coming from the food on the table.

How can I make him stop? All members of the family must cooperate in retraining Clancy to stay off the table. As much as you love Clancy, he needs to learn that there are limits to what you will allow him to do and that you firmly draw the line at having him on the table during meals.

What to say and do Everybody must immediately stop giving Clancy any reward for being on the table. There must be no expression of humor, no matter how funny or charming Clancy may be at that moment. More importantly, Clancy must *never* be given any food from the table—not even one little taste!

When you come home from work, make it a point to kick off your shoes and sit down for a few minutes before starting dinner, and have Clancy join you. He will enjoy being stroked or combed lightly while you unwind from your day. Or spend a few minutes playing with him. Having just a few minutes of your undivided attention while you toss his ball or drag a string around the room for him to chase will go a long way toward making him feel like the important family member he is.

Clancy must be made to stay off the table when you start putting the food on. If nobody can supervise him during this phase, put him in another room. Do not give him the opportunity to reward himself by jumping up on the table and stealing food. When you are ready to sit down to dinner, let Clancy back into the room. Keep an eye on him while you are eating. When he crouches in preparation for jumping on the table, give a *sharp clap* and say in a sharp tone, "No, Clancy! Keep off!" If Clancy jumps up anyway, pick him up and put him back on the floor while saying in a firm voice, "No, Clancy. You are not allowed on the table!" Continue attempting to stop him before he jumps and be very persistent about putting him down when he jumps up.

Some cats catch on very quickly and learn to sit quietly while you eat. Others are more stubborn. After removing Clancy from the table half a dozen times without results, take Clancy out of the room. Say in a firm voice, "I'm sorry, Clancy. We would like to have you with us, but you are making a pest of yourself. If you can't stay off the table, you will have to stay in the other room while we eat." Repeat this routine for as many nights as it takes Clancy to get the message.

Why this works Cats are sociable creatures who like your company. As much as Clancy would like some of your food, he will soon learn that if he wants to stay in the dining room with you, he will have to stay off the table.

Preventative tips Never allow the cat to remain on the table while you are eating, even if you are just having a snack. Never give him any food or allow him to help himself while he is on the table.

Eating dirt

My cat occasionally eats dirt out of my potted plants. She often upsets the plants, which makes a mess for me to clean up, and frequently she vomits up some of the dirt she has eaten, making an even bigger mess. Is there something in the dirt that is making her sick? How can I make her stop eating the dirt out of my plants and making messes by upsetting the pots?

Why is my cat doing this? Cats eat many strange things, including clay litter-box filler and the dirt from potted plants. The activity is called pica, and it can be a sign of illness in cats, especially those with severe anemia. However, often there is no satisfactory explanation for the behavior. It may be that in future years pet food manufacturers will discover some element in these substances that cats need for complete nutrition. In the meantime, make sure that Mewsette is getting a good, wholesome diet of food formulated especially for cats.

The dirt in your plants probably will not harm Mewsette, but you should consider the potential hazard from the chemicals you add. Cats do not have a very good system for eliminating toxins from their bodies, and tiny amounts of common household compounds, such as antifreeze and aspirin, can be deadly to cats.

How can I make her stop? Mewsette may be attracted to the fertilizer you use on your potted plants. Fish-based fertilizer is especially attractive to cats. If you have been using a fish-based fertilizer, consider repotting your plants using new potting mix, and switch to another type of fertilizer.

Vomiting does not always cause cats to avoid the substance they have just eaten. In fact, so many cats eat grass and promptly upchuck that some authorities believe cats eat grass solely for the purpose of cleaning out their stomachs. Mewsette may be using the dirt in your potted plants for the same purpose.

To prevent Mewsette from upsetting your plants, use slightly larger pots and weight them by placing a thick layer of pebbles in the bottom. This will not harm the plants; in fact, the additional drainage afforded by the layer of pebbles will be good for them.

A layer of decorative rock, broken pinecones, or hazelnut shells placed on top of the soil will prevent Mewsette from reaching and licking the potting soil. You can also cover the soil with screening or foil between waterings.

Another way to keep Mewsette out of your planters is to place them where they are inaccessible to her. Shelves that are too high for her to reach from the countertop and too narrow or crowded to offer her a landing spot might work. Small potted plants can be arranged attractively and receive ample light on narrow shelves built into the kitchen window. Larger plants might be suspended from the ceiling in decorative hangers or placed on pedestals that are too high for Mewsette to reach.

Why this works Until scientists learn why cats eat dirt, placing planters out of reach or making them inaccessible by covering the dirt with screening or mulch is the only way to keep your cat out of the plants.

Preventative tips Be extremely careful to read the labels on all the additives you use on your potted plants to ensure that they are not harmful to cats.

Eating the dog's food

We manage to keep the dog from eating the cat's food by feeding the cat on top of the clothes dryer, where the dog can't reach. But we haven't figured out how to keep the cat from eating the dog's food. Will the dog food hurt the cat? How can we make Silver stop taking Bullet's food?

Why is my cat doing this? Cats thrive on well-balanced diets, and many of them eat the same food meal after meal for their entire lives. However, most cats like a fair amount of variety in their diets and will accept a wide range of foods, even such unexpected items as cantaloupe and green beans. In the wild they eat a large variety of small birds and animals and some "vegetables," such as grass. While those with weak stomachs may not want to hear it, cats do eat the digestive tracts of the prey they kill and in so doing, ingest a wide variety of plant food—seeds, berries, and grains.

Aside from that, cats generally just want some of what the other fellow is having. If you offer ten cats ten identical dishes, filled with identical amounts of the same food, the cats will quickly nudge their way into their neighbor's dish. That generally isn't a problem, because that cat has already moved over to his neighbor's dish, and so on. Some cats will try all ten dishes before they settle down to eat. They just want to make sure they aren't missing anything.

Dogs' nutritional requirements are different from what cats need to maintain good health. While there is nothing in Bullet's diet that will harm Silver, he should not be allowed to eat enough of Bullet's food so he isn't hungry for his own well-balanced cat food. The dog food does not contain enough of some elements that Silver needs. Protein content and taurine (an amino acid necessary to prevent blindness and heart disease in cats) are often generally lower in dog food.

How can I make him stop? Generally, dogs are gobblers and cats are nibblers. The easiest solution is to feed Bullet and Silver in separate rooms. You can, with hard work, train Silver to stay out of Bullet's food as long as you are watching, but it is not realistic to expect him to remember to stay away when he gets rewarded with Bullet's food when he raids Bullet's dish. After you leave for work, or when you settle down with your book or TV program, Silver will probably creep in and get into Bullet's food.

What to say and do Continue feeding Silver on top of the clothes dryer, and feed Bullet in the kitchen. After Bullet has had his dinner in peace, you can open the door and allow Silver back inside.

If Bullet was a grazer before you got the cat, accustomed to having his bowl filled in the morning and eating a little all day long, talk to your veterinarian or your dog trainer about teaching him to eat all his food in one or two meals a day. Silver may train Bullet to hurry and finish his food—dogs who live with cats often figure out for themselves that if they do not clean their plates, the cats will do it for them.

Why this works The ideal solution would be to teach Silver to behave like a well-mannered human who respects the rights of others. However, Silver is a cat, not a person, and he will probably continue to raid Bullet's dish every time he has a chance.

Preventative tips Feed your dog and cat in separate rooms to prevent disagreements at mealtimes.

Eating grass

My cat goes outside and eats grass, then comes in the house and throws up on the carpet. Is the grass making her sick? I worry that there is something missing from her diet. I feed her a good brand of canned food twice a day and leave dry food out for her all the time. My veterinarian said she is in good condition and is obviously getting everything she needs from the food I am feeding her. Is there any way to make her stop eating grass?

Why is my cat doing this? Perhaps Chelsea just wants some variety in her diet. One theory is that Chelsea is trying to add folic acid (one of the B vitamins) to her diet. (Some think that cats eat grass in order to vomit to rid themselves of hair balls.) Pet food companies and the American Association of Feed Control Officials (AAFCO)—the independent agency that studies the dietary needs of pets—say that commercially prepared national brands of cat food contain complete and balanced nutrition for all stages of a cat's life, but it is well established that cats enjoy dietary variety. But changing Chelsea's diet could lead to digestive upsets—vomiting and/or diarrhea—and to demands for constant variety. It is better to leave her on the food your veterinarian recommends and offer tidbits (after she eats her regular dinner) for variety.

How can I make her stop? Eating grass will not harm Chelsea, but there is some risk from fertilizers, pesticides, or other chemicals used to treat the lawn, and Chelsea may chew on some plants that are poisonous to her. Even if Chelsea didn't eat grass, she might pick up these substances from a freshly treated lawn on her paws and fur, and ingest them during grooming. The best way to protect Chelsea from accidental poisoning from gardening chemicals is to keep her indoors.

Pet stores offer inexpensive, preplanted containers of grass, especially for cats. These containers do not contain any pesticides or fertilizers that might harm Chelsea and they provide a safe, indoor outlet for her desire for greens. Start growing a second container of greens for Chelsea about two weeks after the grass in the first container has grown to a height of about one inch. If Chelsea enjoys the commercially packaged grass, you will need to replace it in a few weeks. You can also offer Chelsea some alfalfa sprouts, lettuce, cooked green beans, broccoli, or other vegetable to add some greens to her diet. Many cats enjoy leftover steamed vegetables or salad; some also like cantaloupe and watermelon.

Pet food companies carefully balance the nutrients in cat food, so you should be careful about offering Chelsea treats. The general rule is that treats and supplements should be restricted to no more than 10 percent of the total day's food intake to prevent interference with good nutrition. A teaspoon-sized tidbit of chicken, meat, or other people food is a snack for a cat—much more than a teaspoon may interfere with Chelsea's appetite for her regular diet. However, there is no danger of causing an imbalance in Chelsea's diet with fruits and vegetables. These foods are low calorie, low fat, and high fiber, and Chelsea won't eat enough to do her any harm.

Why this works An indoor garden of approved vegetation for your cat will provide her with the "greens" she craves, but eliminates the danger of chemical residues on outdoor plants.

Preventative tips Keep Chelsea indoors where she will be safe from the many dangers of the great outdoors. Your veterinarian will tell you that Chelsea will live a longer, healthier life if you keep her inside.

See also:
Hair balls (fur balls), throwing up
Appendix (Poisons)

Eating houseplants

I used to have a lovely collection of houseplants, but now my cat eats them. She chews on the leaves until they get so ragged and brown that I have to throw them out. Is there anything I can do to make her stop?

Why is my cat doing this? Most cats find houseplants irresistible, but they should not be allowed to eat them. In addition to destroying the plants, the cats could be harming themselves, since many houseplants are poisonous to cats. (See Poisons, in the Appendix). Your veterinarian can supply you with a list of plants that should not be made available to cats. Her or she can also tell you whether Stephanie has any dietary restrictions regarding plants. Cats with a history of bladder or urinary tract conditions might need to be prevented from eating plants. Some cats actually bite off pieces of plants and swallow them, while others just bat them with their paws and chew on them. The plants are both objects of play and perhaps a source of folic acid or fresh greens for the cat's diet.

How can I make her stop? Many cat lovers have only hanging plants. Suspending the plants from the ceiling will move them out of Stephanie's reach. There are a number of commercial cat repellents on the market. Read the label carefully to make sure the product is safe to use in the house. Some of these products are very strong and repel people as well as cats, so you may want to consult a salesperson before you take it home. Scattering orange or lemon peel around the base of the pots or rubbing it on the leaves will may also discourage Stephanie from disturbing the plants.

Provide Stephanie with her own houseplants that she can chew without fear of poisoning or damaging expensive plants. At pet stores you can buy preparations of seed and soil especially selected for cats, or you can make your own. Dig up a small patch of grass from an obscure corner of the yard and place it in a shallow pot for Stephanie or start an indoor grass patch from seed. These kitty gardens need to be replaced fairly often. A fresh batch should be started a week or so after the first, so Stephanie will not run out of grass and revert to the houseplants.

Once Stephanie's personal garden is big enough for her to enjoy (the grass should be about one inch tall), you need to train her to leave your plants alone. When you catch her approaching your plants, pick her up and carry her to her own garden. Say, "Here, Stephanie, this is your garden here. I got this especially for you because I know it will taste better than those old plants of mine." Twitch the blades of grass with your finger to attract her attention. Continue to carry her to her own garden for a few days until she learns that you want her to chew her plants, not yours.

If Stephanie persists in chewing your plants, use stronger measures to discourage her. Use the *magazine toss* every time she approaches your plants. Wait a few seconds, then pick her up and carry her to her garden and say, "Here, Stephanie, this lovely garden is just for you. This is where you come when you want something green to chew."

To keep Stephanie out of the plants when you are away, balance a few *shaker cans* on the rims of the planters. When Stephanie attacks the plants, she will dislodge the cans and frighten herself.

Why this works Stephanie may be chewing your houseplants simply because she wants some fresh greens in her diet. The potted grass satisfies this need. Adding the aversion of the magazine toss and shaker cans makes the houseplants less attractive than her private garden as a place to graze.

Preventative tips Give a new kitten his own garden and discourage plant eating from the beginning, no matter how cute it is.

Exploring dangerous places

O ur five-month-old kitten got into the clothes dryer the other day, and it was just by luck she wasn't killed. As I was putting clothes into the dryer, I thought I saw the kitten out of the corner of my eye. When I looked into the dryer, there she sat! Why would a kitten get into the dryer on a pile of wet clothes? How can I keep her from doing this?

Why is my cat doing this? There is an old English proverb, "Curiosity killed the cat, but satisfaction brought it back." Sadly, this is only half true. While many cats are killed because their curiosity leads them into danger, once they are dead there is no way to satisfy that curiosity and restore the cat to life. Cats love to explore, and they especially love caves, such as the clothes dryer, oven, microwave, refrigerator, and so on. Many cats and kittens are seriously injured every year by jumping into the dryer, refrigerator, or freezer when the owner's back is turned.

There have been reports of cats spending the night in the refrigerator without apparent harm, but these are anecdotal stories, and you should not bet your cat's life on them. The temperature of household refrigerators is usually about 40°F, five degrees colder than the minimum allowed by the U.S. Department of Agriculture for pets that are being shipped by airlines, and the amount of oxygen inside a closed refrigerator is undocumented. Sometimes the cat is rescued because somebody wants a snack at bedtime and opens the refrigerator door, or the cat meows loudly enough for the owner to hear it over the noise of the dryer, and sometimes the owner hears a strange thumping, like the noise made when a tennis shoe is put in the dryer, and opens the door to see what is going on. These are the lucky cats who are released from their accidental prisons before it is too late.

How can I make her stop? Because Mattie has as much awareness of dangerous situations as does a human toddler, you are going to have to make sure she stays out of dangerous places.

What to say and do Mattie is doing what is natural for a cat—exploring. It is anybody's guess why a cat would choose to explore an area filled with cold, damp clothes, but they do. When you are doing laundry, you need to make sure Mattie is out of the room and the door is firmly closed. To be extra safe, after the wet clothes are placed in the dryer and the dryer door is closed, go check on Mattie before you start the dryer. If the door to the dryer is closed and you can see Mattie, that means she isn't in the dryer and it is safe for you to dry your clothes.

No appliance should be started until you are sure it does not contain a cat. Keep the doors to your washer, dryer, oven, dishwasher, and microwave closed when you are not using them. Always double-check to make sure Mattie is not inside before you push the start button.

You can also use a little aversion training to help keep Mattie out of the refrigerator and clothes dryer. Be warned that you are going to have some explaining to do if other family members are at home or if the walls of your apartment aren't completely soundproof. Stand in front of the appliance with the door open. When Mattie gets in, pound on the refrigerator grating or the top of the dryer with your hands and yell "Aieee, yieee, yiee" or "Yip yip yip yip yip" at the top of your lungs while pounding vigorously. The cat will come shooting out of the appliance and may never go back. Many breeders purposely set up these situations in an attempt to train their kittens to steer clear of these life-threatening appliances.

Why this works Cats hate loud noises. It usually takes only one or two encounters with a banging, shrieking appliance to discourage them from future exploration of that particular "cave."

Preventative tips No amount of training in the world will substitute for vigilance. In the same way that you would not allow a three-year-old child to play near a busy street without your immediate attention, you must protect your cat from getting into life-threatening situations.

Fearful, being

Gracie is a beautiful cat, but she is afraid of her own shadow. She runs when the doorbell rings and we don't see her again until hours after the company has left. She is usually loving with our family, but sometimes she runs from us when we walk into a room. What is the matter with her?

Why is my cat doing this? Gracie is a survivor. Cats have survived for thousands of years by being cautious creatures. They are relatively small and are not equipped to win a battle with a large predator, such as a coyote. They have survived by learning to climb trees or by hiding and being very still until the danger has passed. Because your family members are fairly quiet, and because Gracie is alone in a quiet house most weekdays, she is easily startled by sudden noise and movement. When you unexpectedly appear in a room, Gracie doesn't hang around to see whether you are friend or foe. Erring on the side of caution, Gracie bolts for a safe place to hide until the coast is clear.

How can I make her stop? Gracie has an overdose of caution. Since she is kept strictly indoors, she is not in much danger of being eaten by a wolf. You may be walking a little too quickly when you come into a room, or your footsteps may be heavy and rapid enough to frighten her. Cats have excellent eyesight, but Gracie's early warning device sounds the alarm before you are actually in the room, and she dives for cover before she has a chance to see you.

What to say and do Leave a radio or the television on while you are away from home, so Gracie can get accustomed to a little more noise in the house. Try walking more slowly and quietly. Begin speaking several steps before you reach the door to the room where Gracie is. In a cheerful voice say, "Hi, Gracie, I'm home. What have you been doing all day?" Continue talking until you are inside the room and Gracie has had a chance to identify you as a friend. You may feel silly talking to the cat, but she will recognize your voice, and your calm, cheerful tone will notify her that there are no predators lurking nearby.

To overcome Gracie's fear of visitors, have a friend help you retrain her. Put Gracie in her carrier a few minutes before your friend's scheduled arrival. When the doorbell rings, say cheerfully, "Our friends are here, Gracie." Open the door and invite your friend inside. Pick up the carrier and take Gracie with you to where you and your friend will sit and talk. Say, "Betty's here, Gracie. Isn't it nice to have company? What a brave girl you are." Of course Gracie isn't the least bit brave, but she will become more so with practice and encouragement. Have a nice visit with your friend, and shortly after she leaves, take Gracie out of the carrier and pet her and tell her what a good, brave kitty she was. Continue training Gracie, using the carrier every time you expect company. Everybody who loves cats will understand what you are doing. It will take a number of sessions with different friends or groups of friends to train Gracie not to race for shelter every time the doorbell rings. However, if Gracie becomes frantic when she hears the doorbell and realizes she can't get away, resign yourself to having a cat who loves only you and will not tolerate other people. Rather flattering, don't you think? Not every cat is happy in the role of life of the party. Make sure Gracie has an escape route available so she can make graceful exits.

Why this works Often cats who are members of a small, quiet household are shy of strangers. Some warm up in a few minutes, some never do. Cats take their cue from other members of their society. If one cat streaks for cover, every cat in the vicinity will also run. In the absence of other cats, Gracie gets her clues from you. If you are calm and cheerful, obviously there is no danger, so Gracie will feel safe.

Preventative tips Kittens should be handled gently several times a day from the day they are born, and should be raised as family members. When selecting a new kitten, try to find one that was raised in the house and is accustomed to routine household activities.

Feral cats, taming

We caught a half-grown cat who has been living in our woodpile. We would like to keep him, but he seems to hate people. When we come into the room to feed him, he backs into the corner and cowers. When my wife tried to pick him up, he yowled and bit and scratched her. What should we do?

Why is the cat doing this? You are very compassionate people to attempt to rescue the cat, but you may not be able to tame him. Feral cats—those who have never had contact with humans and those who have been abused—are sometimes impossible to tame. Sometimes these cats can be tested for contagious diseases, vaccinated, neutered, and returned to their territory. Cats who are not healthy, and those who are not welcome in the neighborhood, have to be put to sleep.

Even well-socialized cats are sometimes frightened when they are away from their known territory. These cats will hide under the bed or behind the dresser in their new homes until they think it is safe to come out. Some hide for several days or several weeks, emerging only when they are alone in the house, and then only to eat and use the litter box. Some are so badly frightened that they will scratch or bite if you attempt to drag them out of their hiding place.

How can I make him stop? It may not be possible to turn the cat into a pet. Seek professional advice from a local group that works with feral cats.

What to say and do Be extremely cautious with the cat and do not attempt to handle him without expert guidance. If you are determined to try taming the cat, you need professional help. Call your local animal control agency for the names of individuals or groups who are experienced in handling feral cats.

Have the cat examined by your veterinarian as soon as possible to make sure the cat is healthy and is not carrying a virus, fungus, or parasites that may be a threat to you and your family or your other pets.

Why this works There are many groups across the country that work with feral cat colonies in TTVNR (trap, test, vaccinate, neuter, and release) programs. They are experienced at trapping the cats without harm to themselves or the cats. Neutering and releasing healthy individuals helps prevent the birth of more homeless kittens.

Preventative tips Call your local animal control or humane association for help in trapping feral cats.

See also:
Strays, dealing with

Fighting with other cats, indoors

We have spent a lot of time making friends with a stray cat somebody dumped near our house. He has made a drastic adjustment—he even let us give him a bath. We have had him tested, vaccinated, and neutered and would like to make him a part of the family, but he fights with our other cats. He has to live in the utility room because he can't get along. How can we make him behave so he can live in the house with us?

Why is my cat doing this? Living on his own, Bruiser has had to learn to defend himself from other cats. He needs to learn that there is plenty of food and affection for everyone and that inside your house there is no need to fight.

How can I make him stop? Since Bruiser has demonstrated his willingness to be handled by you, even to the extent of having a bath, he is a good candidate for introduction to your household. All that is needed is patience and a lot of affection for all concerned.

What to say and do Change Bruiser's name to something less combative. Although cats don't speak English, Bruiser no doubt senses that you are proud of his ability to defend himself and survive in adverse conditions. Changing his name will help remind you that you want him to live a more gentle life from now on.

Start the introduction slowly. Keep Bruiser (or, now, Cruiser) in the utility room for now, but trade the cats' bedding and toys so they have a chance to become familiar with each other's scents. Place Cruiser's toys and bedding where the other cats play and sleep, and vice versa.

Exchange litter boxes. Instead of dumping and scrubbing the litter boxes, scoop the solids out of the boxes and switch the boxes' places. Urine is perhaps the most important marking device, and this exchange allows the cats to become familiar with each other's scent without direct confrontation.

Allow all the cats to sniff at each other through the closed door. There may be some growling and puffing up for the first day or two, but that should subside as all three cats realize they are safe behind the door that is separating them.

After the growling has stopped, bring Cruiser out for a few minutes of visiting. Keep him on your lap and stroke and talk to him. Say in a calm voice, "What do you think, sweetie? Isn't it nice to be in here with all of us? When you get used to living here so you don't have to growl at the other cats, you can be in here with us all of the time."

Another adult member of the household should hold one or both of your other cats on his or her lap and stroke and talk to them. Say, "Look, girls, here is your new friend. Isn't he a handsome fellow?" Gradually increase the visiting time to about 20 minutes. When the cats are all able to remain relaxed, leave the door to Cruiser's room ajar and allow the cats to mingle. If Cruiser starts acting combative, remind him firmly that he must not fight. Say, "No, Cruiser. We all have to live in harmony. The girls live here, too, and you just have to learn to get along."

If Cruiser doesn't behave, put him back in his room. Say, "Well, Cruiser, I guess it was too soon. We'll try again tomorrow."

Why this works Cruiser acts like he wants to be an indoor cat. Cats learn very quickly what they have to do in order to get what they want.

Preventative tips Always introduce cats slowly and lavish affection on all of them to prevent hurt feelings.

Fighting with other cats, outdoors

Our cat keeps getting in fights with other cats. We have had to take him to the vet twice, once to fix a torn ear and once because he got an abscess from a fight-inflicted wound. He is a nice cat. Why does he keep getting in fights? How can we make him stay closer to home and stop fighting?

Why is my cat doing this? Some neutered cats get in fights with other cats, but generally it is unneutered cats that fight. They fight for territory and for the attention of female cats. Bosworth can smell a female in heat from a considerable distance and is compelled by his hormones to search out the female and try to mate with her. Unfortunately, there are other whole males in the area with the same idea, and they are willing to fight Bosworth for the female's attentions.

How can I make him stop? You have to remove the cause of Bosworth's roaming and fighting. Since you probably are not going to have much success getting your neighbors to spay or neuter their cats, you will have to make the necessary changes.

What to say and do Keep Bosworth indoors and have him neutered. Male cats who are neutered are much more affectionate once their hormones settle down. Without the distraction of the compulsion to mate, Bosworth will be more able to pay attention to you. Neutering males is a relatively uncomplicated surgery, and most cats are acting normally by the following day. The most difficult part of the surgery is enforcing the veterinarian's advice to keep him quiet.

Animals do not experience sexual urges in the same way that humans do. While we control our urges through conscious thought, our pets have no moral or ethical constraints against breeding and are dominated by their hormones. Keeping Bosworth indoors without having him neutered will certainly keep him out of fights, but his behavior will likely not be acceptable to you. When the neighborhood females go into heat, Bosworth will announce his availability by spraying urine in the house. He may also pace and howl and scratch on the doors and windows to be let outside. Some cats actually become ill from sexual frustration, and many of them will lick or bite at themselves until they cause sores and bald spots.

Neutering alone will not end Bosworth's fighting. He will stop fighting over females, and stay closer to home, but he may still engage in battles over territory. Keeping him indoors is the best way to keep him safe. His desire to go outdoors will diminish greatly as the sexual hormones decrease after he is neutered.

Why this works The sexual drive in male cats is excessive. While this is nature's way of ensuring the survival of the species, there are far too many unwanted cats, and the species is in no danger of becoming extinct. Having Bosworth neutered is part of being a responsible pet owner and helping alleviate the pet overpopulation problem.

Keeping Bosworth indoors is best for him. Your veterinarian will tell you of the many health benefits gained by neutering Bosworth and making him into an inside cat. Cats who are neutered and kept indoors live longer, healthier lives.

Preventative tips If you are not planning to breed your cat, have him neutered as soon as your veterinarian says he is old enough. Keep him indoors from the day you get him—cats who have never been outside do not know they are missing anything.

Finicky eater

My cat is so finicky I'm afraid he is going hungry. Sometimes I have to open three or four cans of cat food before I find one he likes. Even when I find one he likes, he will only eat it one or two times, and then he stops liking that food, too. I waste a lot of money throwing out food that Lionel won't eat. I worry that if I have to go out of town he will go hungry because the people at the boarding kennel won't want to go to the trouble to find out what he wants to eat. I put dry food out for him every day, but he ignores it. How can I get my cat to eat like a normal cat?

Why is my cat doing this? Lionel sounds like he just isn't very hungry. Cats like variety in their diets, and Lionel certainly seems to have you trained to provide him with a richly varied diet. Like a small child, Lionel would prefer ice cream and candy to a nourishing meal. Cats usually don't eat a full meal at one sitting. They like to eat a little at a time. If there are no other cats competing for the food, most cats will nibble at their food throughout the day. Lionel is eating enough of his dry food to satisfy his hunger, and in the evening he is full enough to reject one food after another until you give him something interesting enough to gain his attention.

How can I make him stop? You are going to have to be very hard-hearted in order to train Lionel to eat like a normal cat. First, take Lionel to visit the veterinarian to make sure he does not have a medical problem that would make dieting a bad idea.

Before you go to bed, pick up his food dish, dispose of any left-over food, and wash the dish. In the morning, get his clean dish, put in one-third cup of the dry food recommended by your veterinarian and offer it to him. Say cheerfully, "Breakfast is ready, Lionel. Here's some good food for you." Drop the food into the dish so it makes noise. Don't wait to see whether he is interested in the food, but go about your business for about fifteen minutes. After fifteen minutes, go back and look at the dish. Say, "Oh, not hungry this morning, Lionel? All right, you don't have to eat if you aren't hungry." Pick up the dish, put the food back in the container, put the container away, and wash the dish. Be sure to keep him supplied with plenty of clean, fresh water at all times.

Repeat the process in the evening. Get out the good dry cat food, rattle about one-third cupful into his dish and say, "Dinner, Lionel. Come and get it." Walk away and ignore him for about fifteen minutes. Again, come back, and look at the dish. If he has not eaten, or hasn't eaten much, say, "Oh, you aren't hungry, Lionel? That's okay, you don't have to eat if you don't want to." Pick up the dish, put the food back in the container, put the container away, and wash his dish.

On the second day, do exactly as you did on the first day. Offer Lionel the diet that you know is good for him. Ignore his pleas for something good to eat, ignore his plaintive cries, and present the recommended dry food. Give him fifteen minutes to decide whether he wants to eat today, then pick the food up.

Lionel may hold out for as long as three days if he is truly spoiled, but as soon as he is really hungry, he will eat what is offered. Unless Lionel has a health problem, a short fast will not hurt him.

If you want to feed canned food to Lionel, follow the same schedule, but make sure you offer him fresh food at each meal. It would be cruel to expect him to eat canned food that is not fresh.

Why this works Lionel has been eating enough dry food while nobody was looking. He knows if he continues to turn up his nose at the evening offering he will eventually be given something really good to eat. This is a test of wills. If you hold out long enough and continue to offer him only what *you* want him to eat, Lionel will get hungry enough to eat good-quality cat food.

Preventative tips Offer only high-quality cat food and resist the temptation to give Lionel something different the first time he appears uninterested.

Fleas, being attractive to

Our cat has fleas. We have tried everything, but we can't seem to get rid of them for more than a few days. We have bathed him, sent him to the groomer, and had him dipped at the vet's. He even wears a flea collar. Is there something wrong with our cat that makes him attractive to fleas? How can we get rid of them?

Why is my cat doing this? The bad news is that Romeow doesn't have fleas—your house and yard have fleas, and the fleas are getting on your cat. No matter what you do to Romeow, he will continue to have fleas until you eliminate them from your house and yard.

Some cats do seem to be especially attractive to fleas, the same way some people seem to be attractive to mosquitoes, but if your yard and house are free of fleas, there won't be any to get on Romeow. Feeding Romeow a little brewer's yeast, available from health food stores, may make him a little less delectable but won't get the fleas out of your carpet and grass.

How can I make him stop? Collars in general are dangerous unless they are especially designed to break away if they get snagged, and flea collars contain poison.

There is no easy way to eliminate fleas. It is hard work and may take several applications to completely rid your house and yard of fleas, but it can be done and it is worth the effort. There are many great new products on the market. Check with your veterinarian to see what products she or he recommends.

Flea control involves the use of poisons. Read and follow the manufacturer's directions on all chemicals and store them out of the reach of children and pets. Spray your yard, paying special attention to the areas near the front and back doors. Fleas will hop on the cuffs of your pants and your socks and hitch a ride into the house. Use Diazinon, a relatively benign pesticide available in garden stores. Follow the manufacturer's directions carefully. Although this is a "safe" poison, it is still a poison. Keep your pets off the lawn until it is dry. Ask your veterinarian about the new nonchemical yard spray that is safe for pets, birds, and people.

Spray one room, such as the bathroom, with the environmental product recommended by your veterinarian. This is the "clean" room where you will put Romeow after his bath so the other fleas living in your house can't hop on him.

Bathe Romeow in a veterinarian-recommended flea shampoo for cats. Rinse him thoroughly and put him in the bathroom to dry.

Spray the vacuum cleaner bag with the environmental flea control product, so fleas will be killed when you vacuum them up, and vacuum the whole house, including around the baseboards, even in uncarpeted rooms. Following the manufacturer's instructions, spray the whole house with the environmental product, around all the baseboards, under the bed, under the couch, and between the cushions. Leave the house for an hour.

Because it is impossible to kill fleas during the pupae stage, more fleas will emerge over a period of ten days. Plan to repeat the process every other week for eight weeks to completely eliminate fleas, then every three to six months, if needed.

If your yard is not fenced, neighborhood dogs, cats, and possibly raccoons and squirrels will wander through and drop fleas in your yard for your dog and cat to pick up later. Check with your veterinarian about products to help prevent reinfestation and ask about Program, a revolutionary new flea control product.

Why this works Your cat is not the cause of the flea problem but is one of the primary victims of the infestation. A thorough extermination program is the only way to rid your cat, home, and yard of fleas.

Preventative tips Keep Romeow indoors so he won't wander into areas visited by flea-infested animals. If your yard is not fenced, spray twice a year, especially around entryways, to keep hitchhikers from riding indoors on your clothing.

Grooming, objecting to

Snowflake is a beautiful, pure white longhaired cat, but she hates to be combed. She bites and scratches us when we try to comb out her tangles. Twice we have had to take her to the vet because her fur became so matted that she had to be shaved. How can we make her behave so we can comb her?

Why is my cat doing this? There are several things Snowflake may dislike about being groomed. You may be holding her too tightly because you expect her to object. If her hair is tangled, it probably hurts when you comb through it, or the comb may be the wrong kind and may catch and pull Snowflake's hair.

How can I make her stop? Since your veterinarian has examined Snowflake, he no doubt looked to see if there was a medical reason, such as an abscess or other sore spot, for her objection to being combed. Snowflake needs a gentle reintroduction to grooming. With the proper tools and a loving, gentle approach, you should be able to teach Snowflake not only to tolerate grooming, but to enjoy it as an extra session of affection.

What to say and do Make one more trip to the groomer and let the professional get Snowflake's coat combed out. Ask the groomer to use a feline cream rinse to reduce tangling and ask about the comb or brush she uses and get one like it to use at home.

While Snowflake is still looking perfect from her trip to the beauty parlor, before she has a chance to develop snarls and tangles in her fur, start teaching her to accept being groomed by you. Put Snowflake on the counter or your lap, where you normally try to groom her. Show her the comb while you pet her and talk quietly to her. Say, "Look, Snowflake, we got you a new comb. We are going to have such a nice time keeping you all pretty with this new comb." Pick up the comb and lightly stroke under her chin and on top of her head with it. If it is necessary to restrain Snowflake, just circle her with your arm or lay your hand gently on her shoulders or chest. Gently grasp her tail and run the comb through the fur on the end, combing in the same direction the hair grows and being careful not to pull. If you hit a tangle, stop immediately. Grasp that section of hair close to Snowflake's skin, and hold it firmly, without pulling, and gently comb the hair that protrudes from your hand.

If Snowflake objects, stop combing her tail and scratch her chin and ears with your hand. Say, "Oh, I didn't mean to pull. I'm sorry." Then, again, stroke her throat, chin, and head with the comb. When Snowflake relaxes, start combing gently again.

Keep the sessions very short, and keep your touch very light. Cats "frown" with their ears, so watch Snowflake's ears and stop combing when she lowers them. Say, "I'm sorry, honey, I didn't mean to pull." Keep these sessions very short. Do a little every day or twice a day. At the end of the session, praise her, even if the session lasted only 30 seconds. Say in a cheerful voice, "What a brave girl. Don't you look pretty all combed."

Why this works Cats engage in mutual grooming to show their affection. Some cats even groom their owners. Keeping the sessions short, avoiding pain, and cheering Snowflake along will make her grooming sessions a pleasurable event.

Preventative tips Start grooming kittens before they need it. Make daily combing or brushing a part of a relaxing, pleasant time together. Let Snowflake know that you are grooming her because it pleases you, not because it is a chore that has to be done.

Hair balls (fur balls), throwing up

My cat doesn't seem to be sick, but she occasionally vomits up wads of hair. Sometimes she coughs before she throws up. Why is she throwing up? Is there any way to keep her from doing this?

Why is my cat doing this? Cats and other fur-bearing mammals, including humans, shed dead hairs throughout the year. Cats ingest this fur during grooming. Usually this small amount of hair passes harmlessly through the cat's digestive system, but during the heavy shedding season of spring, Moonbeam will shed a great deal of hair. Cats are unable to spit out hair, and when she is shedding heavily Moonbeam swallows more hair than can be easily passed through her system. Vomiting is nature's way of helping her expel this extra hair so it won't block her intestines. The coughing that is sometimes seen just before a hair ball is vomited up is believed to be caused by pressure from the hair ball.

How can I made her stop? You can help Moonbeam by removing the extra hair before she licks it off and by giving her a small amount of lubricant to assist the hair in passing through her digestive tract.

What to say and do Bathe Moonbeam and rinse her in running water an extra-long time to wash as much loose hair as possible down the drain. Hold the spray nozzle against Moonbeam's skin, moving it against the grain of her coat to loosen dead hair. After Moonbeam is dry, comb out the loosened hair and comb her several times a day for the next two or three days to eliminate all the hair that was loosened by her bath.

Increase weekly combing or brushing sessions to daily sessions during the spring and summer and spend a little extra time removing dead hair.

Ask your veterinarian about giving Moonbeam a hair-ball remedy at this time to help the swallowed hair pass through her digestive tract. These preparations are available from your veterinarian, pet shops, and grooming shops. They are lubricants—such as petroleum jelly with a flavoring, such as malt, to make them palatable to cats—and are sold under brand names like Petromalt, Femalt, Kittylax, Laxitone, and others.

Moonbeam may like the taste of the preparation enough to lick it off your finger, or you may have to use a little force. If Moonbeam doesn't want the remedy, you can rub it onto the roof of her mouth or rub it into the fur on the front of her leg. Smear the lubricant down the front of her leg in a fairly thin film. If you just stick on a clump of it, she will simply shake her leg and fling it across the room.

Why this works Moonbeam's system is just trying to stay healthy by vomiting up what can't be digested. Hair-ball remedies lubricate the hair and help it pass through the system. Helping Moonbeam rid herself of excess hair will prevent it from accumulating into an indigestible mass in her stomach.

Preventative tips Routine grooming, especially during the spring and summer months, will remove excess hair and help prevent hair balls.

See also:
Vomiting

Heat, constant

My Himalayan seems to be in constant heat. She meows all the time and is getting very thin because she hardly eats. She is almost two years old and I would like to breed her. I have her papers, but I can't find anyone with a Himalayan stud who is willing to breed her. I want her to have at least one litter so she will settle down. Where can I find a breeder who will give me stud service?

Why is my cat doing this? Cats cycle far more frequently than do dogs. While most dogs have heat cycles once or twice a year, female cats go in and out of heat all year long. It is common for domestic cats to cycle ten days on and ten days off from early spring until late fall, and continue to cycle, although less frequently, during the winter months. Kahlua will settle down as she becomes more mature. There is nothing associated with the physical aspects of gestation, birth, and lactation that causes an individual to grow up.

How can I make her stop? Breeding Kahlua will not make her stop being in heat, except during the nine weeks she is pregnant. Many cats go back into heat while they are still nursing their kittens. The permanent way to end the heat cycle is to neuter Kahlua. Nor will having a litter make Kahlua calm down. The myth that having a litter causes cats to settle down is perpetuated because the birth of kittens so often coincides with the cat's entry into adulthood. As Kahlua leaves kittenhood behind, she will naturally become more mature in her behavior.

What to say and do Registration papers only prove what breed the cat is and do not reflect whether the cat is a suitable candidate for breeding. Get in touch with the breeder who sold Kahlua to you. If she sold Kahlua to you as a breeding cat, she should offer you her assistance and guidance in the selection of a stud, based on Kahlua's pedigree and physical characteristics. Because she is familiar with the characteristics of Kahlua's ancestors, the original breeder is the best person to determine whether Kahlua is a good candidate for breeding and what lines or individual studs have the best chance of producing top-quality kittens with her. Talk to her frankly about stud fees, expenses for veterinary care, and the difficulty of finding homes for the kittens.

Breeding cats is a very expensive hobby. Without the assistance of an established breeder, you are going to have a very hard time finding a breeder to offer stud service for Kahlua. Breeders are very protective of the health of their cats and are not willing to allow contact with cats belonging to people they do not know. In the unlikely event you are able to find a stud for Kahlua, the fee will be very high. By the time you pay the stud fee and have the kittens tested and vaccinated, your costs will have far outreached anything you might gain by selling the kittens. A quick glance at the classified ads in your local paper will show you that kittens do not command prices high enough to offset your costs.

Your best course of action is to accept Kahlua for the beautiful companion she is and have her spayed to end the upsetting heat cycles.

If you are really interested in breeding, visit a local cat show and talk to the breeders and exhibitors. Buy a show-quality kitten and enter her in shows. In the course of showing your kitten, you will meet many other cat lovers and acquire a wealth of information on cat behavior, genetics, and health.

Why this works Spaying, the removal of the uterus and ovaries, completely and permanently removes the cause of heat in female cats.

Preventative tips Bringing a kitten into your home is a long-term commitment. Don't buy a kitten with the idea that you can have "just one litter" to offset the purchase price. Choose a kitten that you think will become a valuable friend and companion in its own right.

Indoors, keeping

We have just moved from a quiet neighborhood where we felt safe letting Raggs go outside to a house on a busy street. We think the street is too dangerous to allow Raggs outdoors, but he doesn't want to stay in. He cries and scratches at the door to be let out. When we don't open the door for him, he gets mad and swats one of the other cats. Is there any way to make him settle down and stay inside?

Why is my cat doing this? Raggs has always gone outside and does not understand that his new confinement is for his own safety. Outside is much more interesting than inside. Raggs understands your authority and knows that he cannot smack you to display his anger, so he redirects it at a safe target—one of the other cats.

How can I make him stop? Do not, under any circumstances, open the door and let Raggs out. Raggs is a smart cat, and it only takes one success to convince him that if he begs long enough, scratches vigorously enough, and beats up on the other cats, you will eventually open the door for him.

Make indoors more interesting for Raggs, give him some extra attention to let him know he isn't being punished, and help him work off some of his energy with interactive toys.

What to say and do Hold to your belief that Raggs is safer in the house. A positive attitude about what you are doing will help everybody through the adjustment period.

Try to give Raggs as many of the joys of the outside world as you can. A pot of kitty greens from the pet store or grass from your yard will provide him with one of the elements. A table pushed against the window with a comfortable pillow or a towel to recline on will allow him to see some of what is going on out there, and a bird feeder hung just outside his window will attract birds to entertain him.

Give him a good, sturdy scratching post to exercise his claws on. Make sure it is tall enough for him to stretch his full length and sturdy enough so it won't tip over when he scratches with vigor. Several scratching posts of the many varieties available in pet stores will give him a little of the diversity he enjoyed outside and are a minor investment when you consider the cost of your furniture.

Raggs probably liked jumping up on the fence or climbing trees at his old home. A multilevel scratching tree will provide him with a desirable off-the-floor perch. Hide a catnip toy or two in his new "tree" for him to discover when he jumps up.

Help Raggs run off some of his extra energy by playing with him. Jingle balls, wads of crumpled paper, or one of the fishing pole–type devices that simulate birds or insects can help you exercise him. Few cats can resist a kitty tease when you drag or flick it around for them.

When Raggs goes to the door and cries and scratches to be let out, say, "No, Raggs. You can't go outside. It is too dangerous." Distract him with the kitty tease or some other interesting toy or pick him up and carry him into another room. Continue to discourage him until he stops asking.

For the ultimate compromise, build Raggs an open-air run, or screen in a porch where he can be out of the house, surrounded by nature on three sides, while protected by his screened enclosure.

Why this works Cats are adaptable. Raggs may have enjoyed the great outdoors, but he will eventually come to accept the reality of his new life indoors.

Preventative tips Cats live longer, healthier lives when they are kept indoors. Keep your cat safely in the house. If they are never allowed outside, they will not know the difference.

Jealousy

Our cat seems jealous of our new baby. She jumps up and tries to get in the middle when we are feeding or diapering the baby. Sometimes she paws at the bottle and sticks her nose under our hands as though she were trying to get the nipple. She is becoming a real nuisance with her constant demands for attention when we are trying to care for the baby. How can we get her to understand that we have to take care of the baby?

Why is my cat doing this? Celeste's world has been a little chaotic lately. One of her people has been gone for several days and the other has just run in and out and hasn't had a moment to spare for her. On top of that, now that everybody is home, there is this new member of the household and everybody is still too busy and too tired to give Celeste any attention. Celeste is curious about this new creature that has come into her life, and she is probably a little concerned that you will stop loving her. The baby's formula probably smells interesting, and Celeste would like a taste to make sure she is not missing out on a treat.

How can I make her stop? Celeste needs to have a good look at the baby to learn what sort of creature it is, and she needs to be reassured that she still has a place in your home and your affections. Introducing Celeste to the baby, and making Celeste the center of attention for a few minutes each day, will help her adjust to the changes.

What to say and do A proper introduction will start things off on the right foot. With the baby fed, warm, and dry, get Celeste dressed up for the occasion. Comb or brush Celeste and say, "We have a new member in our family, Celeste. We are going to get all cleaned up nice so we look our best when we meet him. Oh, you look very pretty today, Celeste. The baby is going to be very impressed that he is living with such a gorgeous cat." Keep your tone light and chatty. Go get the baby and sit on the couch and call Celeste. Say, "Celeste, come meet Bryce," and pat the couch invitingly so she jumps up. Display the baby to Celeste just the way you would if Celeste were a small child who had never seen a baby before, showing her his tiny fingers and letting her touch him with her nose. Stroke Celeste and tell her how much Bryce likes her. Say, "Bryce thinks you are beautiful, Celeste."

Invite Celeste to sit with you when you feed the baby. Pat the couch beside you and say, "Come, keep me company while I feed the baby, Celeste." Talk to her during these sessions to make her feel that she is a part of things. "Babies certainly need to be fed a lot, don't they, Celeste? Remember when you were a tiny kitten and all you knew how to do was eat and sleep? It is nice that you are so grown up now and can do more interesting things."

Give Celeste your undivided attention for a few minutes each day. A daily grooming session will help maintain the special bond between you. Tossing a jingle ball for her to chase or playing with a fishing pole—type toy with a cat lure tied to a string will help run off some of her extra energy and relieve any stress she might be feeling. These toys can be found in pet stores or through advertisements in cat magazines.

Why this works Cats and babies are not natural enemies, but it is natural for Celeste to be a little jealous and curious about any new family member, be it human or animal. A cheerful introduction and individual attention let Celeste know that you are happy and that she has no cause for concern. Allowing her to inspect the baby will assure her that it is a harmless creature that she need not fear.

Preventative tips Before the next baby comes, gradually decrease the amount of time you spend with Celeste, while emphasizing the quality of the reduced time together. With any lifestyle change, explain things to Celeste as you go, even if you don't think she understands your words. Your positive attitude conveys itself to Celeste and reassures her that these changes are good.

Jumping, on counter

My cat jumps up and walks all over the kitchen counter, even when there is no food up there. Sometimes she takes a nap on the countertop. Is there any way to keep her off?

Why is my cat doing this? The kitchen counter is a place that is especially attractive to cats. Your cat knows that the countertop is where food is prepared and that there is a good chance she can snatch a treat. It is also off the floor, and cats like to be in high places.

What to say and do If you are at the counter and see your cat preparing to jump, stomp your foot and say in a stern voice, "No,

Sarah! Get away!" Nudge her away from the base of the counter with your foot. If she jumps up anyway, again say sternly, "No!" followed by a *hiss,* and put her on the floor. Be persistent.

If you are not near the counter, shout, "No, Sarah!" and use a *sharp clap.* If she does not get off the counter immediately, pick her up and say, "Sarah! Stay off the counter!" and put her on the floor. Speak loudly and sharply to let her know you are annoyed with her. Do not allow her to remain on the counter. The next time Sarah gets on the counter, spray her with the *squirt bottle.* If she doesn't jump down when you spray her, use the *magazine toss.*

To keep Sarah off the counter while you are away from home, set traps with the *shaker can.* Place about a dozen shaker cans on their sides on the counter and cover them with sheets of newspaper. When Sarah jumps on the counter, she will cause the shaker cans to roll around and make scary noises. You can also cover the countertops with sopping wet towels. A few squishy landings will convince her that the countertop is not a very comfortable place to be.

Once you decide to train Sarah to stay off the counter, you must be consistent and persistent. You must correct the behavior every time it happens. If she is being particularly stubborn and you become too tired to continue the battle of the wills, put her in another room for a while. Do not, under any circumstances, allow her to win by letting her stay on the counter.

Why this works Cats do not hunt in packs, but they do live in hierarchical societies, both in nature and in multicat households. Your cat will recognize you as top cat and do what you want only if you are persistent. Placing her on the floor, or scooting her away from the area with your foot, illustrates to her exactly what you want from her.

Preventative tips Never, never allow your cat to eat anything while she is on the counter. Most especially, never give her a treat or any favorable attention while she is on the counter. The height of the counter, all by itself, is attractive enough to her; giving her food or affection while she is on the counter only reinforces her desire to jump up.

Jumping, on furniture

We would like Sheba to stay off the furniture. She knows we don't want her on the couch and chairs, and she doesn't get on them when we are in the room, but if we go somewhere we find cat hairs on the furniture when we come home. Sometimes she even gets on the furniture when we are just in the next room, although she quickly jumps down when she hears us coming. How can we make her stay off all the time?

Why is my cat doing this? Sheba likes your furniture for the same reason you do—it is more comfortable than the floor and it is somewhat elevated and therefore a little safer. She has taken note of your claim on the furniture and is respecting your position as top cat by allowing you to have it when you want it. What she doesn't understand is why she can't have it when you aren't using it. In cat colonies, the cats who are higher up the pecking order have their preferred spots. The other cats respect this and stay off these spots during the times the top cats are using them, but at other times of the day the lower-ranked cats do use these places, which they immediately yield when the top cats approach. This is what Sheba is doing.

How can I make her stop? Offer Sheba several comfortable places of her own and make the couch uncomfortable for her when you can't be in the room, or cover it to keep the cat hair off.

What to say and do You have already let Sheba know that you are not pleased with her when she gets on your couch or chair. She understands "Get down," but "Stay off" is an elusive concept with no corollary in cat language.

A twofold compromise can quickly put an end to the battle over the couch. Provide Sheba with a padded window perch or a tree house–type scratching post so she has her own spot that is safely up off the floor. If the only problem you have with Sheba's attraction to the furniture is the cat hair she deposits on them, toss a sheet over the furniture at bedtime and remove it when you come home from work. Or place a towel with a color that contrasts sharply with the upholstery on her favorite piece of furniture, and remove it when you want to sit there. Cats are particularly fond of well-defined spaces and will happily curl up on an offered towel or in a shallow box.

To keep Sheba off the furniture completely, invest in a Scat Mat. This device gives a nonharmful but quite unpleasant electric shock when touched. One or two of these highly distasteful encounters will soon convince Sheba that there are more comfortable places to nap.

Why this works Some people do not want their pets on the furniture for aesthetic reasons, and the Scat Mat is a quick, sure way to discourage this activity. Cats are fond of defined spaces and will usually choose to lie in a shallow box or on a towel that contrasts with the upholstery, if these choices are offered. Lounging spots such as a padded window seat or a perch on top of a scratching post are especially attractive because they are somewhat higher off the ground than the furniture, and therefore safer from predators. One, or a combination, of these compromises will keep the cat hair off the furniture without causing you and Sheba undue frustration.

Preventative tips Provide your cats with comfortable places of their own when you bring them into your home. Let them know right away if there are places where they are not allowed and strictly and consistently enforce your rules.

Jumping, on high places

Truffle has a fixation on the top of the hutch, which is eight feet off the floor. She gets up there, winds her way between my display of antique plates and vases, and often curls up for a nap. I'm worried that she is going to knock something off. Is there any way to keep her off the top of the hutch?

Why is my cat doing this? Truffle is demonstrating one of the techniques that has enabled cats, who are fairly small creatures, to survive in the wilderness. By getting on top of the hutch, Truffle is out of reach of the wolves and coyotes. In fact, predators most likely won't even see her if she stays still. This holdover from the behavior of her wild ancestors is still necessary. If Truffle is ever accidentally left outside, she might need the instinct that guides her to the safety of a tall fence or a branch that is well out of the reach of neighborhood dogs. Jumping onto tall furniture or countertops also saves her from the unwanted attention of the family dog and small human visitors.

How can I make her stop? There is no way to eliminate Truffle's instinct to seek the high ground when she feels threatened, but you can discourage her from lounging on top of your hutch and endangering your valuable collection. Let her know that you don't want her up there and make it uncomfortable for her when she does make it to the top.

What to say and do Clear off the top of the hutch and put the fragile china in a temporary safe spot. Place several lightweight magazines and a spray bottle or squirt gun filled with water within easy reach. Stick strips of double-faced masking tape all over the top of the hutch so there is no way Truffle can walk around without stepping on it. When you catch Truffle on top of the hutch, use the *magazine toss* or *spray bottle* to add to her discomfort. If you are in the room and see Truffle crouching, preparing to jump, yell, "No, Truffle! Don't you jump up there! That's my spot!" and use the *sharp clap*. If you are very close to her, use the *hiss* and push her off the table.

If Truffle doesn't get the message in a relatively short time, cover the top of the hutch with crumpled newspaper and balance *shaker cans* precariously on top of each wad of paper. Use enough shaker cans so Truffle is sure to dislodge some of them no matter how graceful she is. Continue to replace the crumpled newspaper and shaker cans as often as she disturbs them.

When the trap has been untouched for several days, replace the booby trap with unfolded paper napkins. Lay the napkins loosely around the perimeter of the hutch and check each morning and evening to see whether they have been disturbed. If the napkins are disturbed, repeat the use of the shaker cans, this time for several days longer than the first time. Truffle may be quite stubborn about this—you have to be more tenacious than she is.

Why this works Cats hate having things stick to their paws and their fur. The double-faced tape makes the top of the hutch an uncomfortable place to walk or lounge. The tone of your voice and the hiss and sharp clap let Truffle know your are displeased with her. While cats don't acknowledge a pack leader, as dogs do, they do live in hierarchical societies and make some effort not to displease the top cat. Finally, the shaker cans, magazine toss, and spray bottle startle Truffle and will help her decide that the top of the hutch may be high off the ground, but it is not a very secure refuge.

Preventative tips Correct unwanted behavior the first time and every time it happens. Lack of immediate action allows bad habits to form and makes retraining more difficult and prolonged.

Jumping, over fences

We want Oscar to stay in our yard. We have a six-foot fence, but he jumps over it with no effort at all and wanders around the neighborhood. We are worried about him getting hit by a car or chased by dogs. Also, the neighbor complains that he uses her flower beds for his bathroom. How can we make Oscar stay in his own yard?

Why is my cat doing this? Oscar is displaying the nature of the cat. Cats who are allowed outdoors have a territory, generally shared more or less peaceably with other neighborhood cats, of up to several blocks. Oscar probably has a daily route he follows—go over the fence to Mrs. Blattner's for a potty stop in the nice, loose soil of her flower bed; stop in at Millie's to see if she left any salmon scraps for him; stroll along the Coopers' fence and make the dogs bark; stop for a drink at the Cruzes' fishpond and see how the goldfish are coming along; and eventually go back home for a nap.

You are right to be concerned about Oscar's rambling. Some of the neighbors are sure to be annoyed, and the exposure to dogs, cars, and other perils is a real danger to his health and safety.

How can I make him stop? If Oscar is not already neutered, have your veterinarian perform this surgery immediately. Among the other benefits, neutering will also encourage Oscar to stay closer to home.

Try leash-training Oscar and allow him to join you while you do your gardening and explore the neighborhood as your companion. Be sure to use a harness designed especially for cats, rather than trying to control him with a collar and lead. Cats either slip out of their collars or choke themselves trying to get out. If you approach Oscar's introduction to the harness with patience and good humor, you are most likely to be successful. Do not leave the leash attached to Oscar's harness unless you have hold of the other end.

If you want to allow Oscar into your yard without human supervision, you need to redesign it so it will contain him. It is difficult to make your fence tall enough so Oscar can't climb or jump over it with the greatest of ease, and many cities have ordinances that set a limit on the height of fences. Check building supply stores for tilt-in fence tops, an extra section of fencing, generally constructed of wire strands or mesh, that fits on top of the existing fence but tilts inward. The angle of the addition denies Oscar his usual escape route, which was to jump to the top of the fence and gather himself before dropping into the neighbor's yard or onto the public sidewalk. The wire is far too unstable to offer Oscar even a temporary perch. Be sure to trim any sturdy shrubs and tree limbs away from the fence so Oscar can't use them to bypass your new barrier.

Another alternative is to construct an open-air enclosure with access through a window. An outdoor run of hardware cloth or chicken wire will allow Oscar to enjoy the fresh air and an expanded view of the world, while keeping him safe and preventing him from annoying the neighbors.

Why this works Leash training and direct supervision is the sure way to keep Oscar out of trouble while allowing him some limited exploring and the pleasure of your company. Many cats like to roam the neighborhood and pretend to be jungle cats, but they often will settle for the safety and companionship of a walk around the block or a session in the garden.

Preventative tips Start by never allowing your kitten outside unattended. Build a window perch or an outside run to allow him to view the outdoors without danger to himself. Have cats neutered as early as possible to reduce roving.

See also:
Walking on leash, resistance to

Kneading

My legs are all scraped from my cat using me for a scratching post. Colleen won't just sit or lie on my lap and watch television with me; she has to make biscuits. No matter what I do, she stands or sits and digs her claws into my knees until I push her off. I like having her on my lap, but I don't like feeling like a pincushion. How can I make her stop sticking her claws into me?

Why is my cat doing this? Kneading is a behavior that most cats indulge in when they are content. The rhythmic pushing and pulling, which is usually accompanied by purring, is thought to be a carryover of the activity kittens use to cause more milk to flow from their mother when they are nursing. Cats have also been observed making these kneading motions on objects they are about to lie on, possibly in an effort to fluff them up and make them more comfortable.

How can I make her stop? Colleen probably isn't going to stop kneading your knees, but you can make the attention less painful by clipping her claws and by providing a buffer between her feet and your tender knees.

What to say and do Buy a pair of nail clippers designed just for cats. You can use human nail clippers for this chore, but having the right equipment makes the job easier and reduces the chances of hurting Colleen. Removing the worry about catching her paw pad in the clipper or pulling the hair around her toes will help you relax.

If you are really concerned about your ability to clip Colleen's nails, have a professional groomer, your veterinarian, or your veterinarian's technician demonstrate the technique for you.

Place Colleen on your lap with her head pointed away from you. Extend Colleen's claw by gently lifting her paw and pressing the pad with your index finger while pulling lightly back with your thumb on top of the paw. Don't hold Colleen's paw with any more force than is necessary to position the claw for clipping. Look to see where the pink vein ends just before the curve of the claw. Place the clipper outside of the vein and snip the tip off the claw.

It is helpful if an assistant distracts Colleen from what is happening by gently scratching her ears and under her chin or by dangling a string or toy in front of her while you work.

Praise Colleen for her bravery. Say, "Aren't you just the bravest, smartest kitty in the world. Look at you, sitting here so nicely to get your manicure. Oh, my, you are going to look wonderful with your nails done." If Colleen is very resistant, just do one or two claws at a time. There is no profit in forcing her to submit and turning each session into a battle of wills. A slow, gentle approach will help her understand that no harm comes from what you are doing. When you have finished, a small treat is in order as a reward for her bravery. Get into the habit of placing a folded towel or small rug on your lap as a buffer between you and Colleen's claws. When Colleen's claws get long enough to start snagging the towel, you will know it is time to give her another manicure.

Why this works A manicure won't stop Colleen's kneading behavior, but it will end the damage to your skin.

Preventative tips Start clipping claws on kittens when they are very young. Start by simply holding their paws gently and extending the claw and rubbing it with your fingers to get them accustomed to having you handle them. Your positive attitude will help kittens accept without fear what you are doing.

Licking hair

My cat has a fixation about my hair. At night he gets up on my pillow and licks and chews on my hair. If I move my head he sinks his claws into my head and bites me. Sometimes he bites me and thumps me on the head with his back feet. Even when he isn't licking my hair, he wants to lie on it, and he gets very upset if I move. What is it about my hair that makes him behave like this? How can I get him to stop giving me so much attention?

Why is my cat doing this? Alexander is grooming you. He bites and thumps you the same way he would if you were a squirmy kitten. Mothers frequently bite and thump kittens to let them know they will not tolerate any nonsense during the bath. Be sure to keep his claws clipped so you won't be injured if he slips. The positive side of this habit is that cats groom only those animals and people they really like. However, a little grooming goes a long way.

How can I make him stop? Try using a different brand of shampoo, rinse, and hair spray to see if Alex is just crazy about those products rather than your hair. If it really is your hair he is after, and not just the good-smelling grooming products, Alex will have to be trained not to groom you.

Make up your mind that you want Alex to stop licking and lying on your hair. You can't train him to lick just a little, or to lie there for just a few minutes and then go elsewhere to sleep. You can allow him to continue as he has in the past or you can train him to stop completely—there is no in-between.

What to say and do Rinse your hair in lemon or vinegar. The rinse will make your hair shine, and the taste will be unpleasant to Alex. This simple act may be enough to end Alex's addiction.

If lemon or vinegar doesn't discourage Alex, offer him his own pillow. If there is another person sharing your bed, place a pillow on the nightstand, or on a chair near the bed. That way Alex can indulge in half of his pleasure—sleeping close to your face—without driving you crazy. When Alex approaches the head of the bed, pick him up and place him on his pillow. Say cheerfully, "Here is your very own pillow, Alex. Isn't this nice? Now you can be close to me and we will both be comfortable." You must be resolutely consistent. Do not allow him to stay on your pillow for even a moment—remove him immediately and put him on his own pillow. Say, "No, Alex, I don't like you on my head. Lie on this nice pillow." Alex may have to be moved onto his pillow a dozen times before he gets the message.

If Alex won't accept your kind offer of another pillow, just push him off when he gets on your head. Don't even wait for him to lie down or start licking—just give him a shove toward the foot of the bed. Say in a stern voice, "No, Alex. Get off my head. It hurts when you pull my hair." Push him down every time he gets up.

At this point Alex may concede and curl up by your side or in the crook of your knee, or he may be exceptionally determined. If he won't stop when you push him away, push him completely off the bed. Say, "Get off, Alex. You can't stay on the bed if you insist on standing on my head!"

When you have tired of pushing him off the bed, get up and put him out of the room. Say, "I'm sorry, Alex, but I can't sleep with you on my head. You'll just have to stay out until you learn to behave." Repeat the exercise every night until Alex finally caves in and agrees to stay out of your hair.

Why this works As much as Alex loves your hair, it is only a part of the whole, wonderful person you are. He wants to be near you, and if he has to give up his fixation on your hair to stay close to you, he will.

Preventative tips Don't let kittens get away with behavior that will be unacceptable when they are adults. If you wouldn't want a twelve-pound cat standing on your head, licking your hair, stop him before it becomes a habit.

See also:
Appendix (Clipping Claws)

Licking people

Berkeley just has one bad habit—he likes to lick my face. When we settle down for the night he starts washing my face, especially my nose and chin. He has licked me so much at times that my nose and chin are raw. I don't want to be mean to him, but it hurts. How can I make him stop?

Why is my cat doing this? Cats groom other cats, the family dog, and human family members both as a sign of affection and, judging by the amount of purring that accompanies this activity, for emotional comfort. Some cats are content with two or three brief I-love-you licks on the hands or face, while others, like Berkeley, overindulge. The intensity of the behavior in these cats is almost that of a nursing kitten and may be an effort to recapture the sense of well-being they knew at that age. Berkeley's licking is the equivalent of thumb-sucking—something he does to relax and fall asleep.

How can I make him stop? Licking your face is a fairly well established habit, but one that can be overcome with persistence. You must steel yourself to be just a little more stubborn than Berkeley on this issue. Correct Berkeley's excessive licking with a two-step approach. Make licking your face unpleasant for him and give him more attention and affection outside the bedroom.

What to say and do Spend a few minutes each evening tossing a ball or paper wad for Berkeley to chase or play with him with a toy on a string to help him exercise away the energy he has built up during the day. Focusing your attention on Berkeley will help reassure him of your affection.

Just before bedtime, spend ten or fifteen minutes grooming Berkeley. Talk to him in a soothing voice during the session and comb and pet him gently. What you say doesn't matter much, as long as he has your attention. Say something like "How was your day, Berkeley? I see you kept all the mice out of the house. Did you see any interesting birds today?" Just chat away while you are petting and combing.

Wring out a cloth or cotton ball in vinegar, lemon juice, or nail polish remover and place it near your face. Or rinse your face with lemon juice or vinegar just before bedtime so you will taste bad. When you get in bed and Berkeley starts to lick your face, immediately push his head away and say in a stern voice, "No, Berkeley! Don't lick me. I don't like it." When he tries to lick you again, push him away again and say, "Stop it, Berkeley. That hurts. I don't want you to lick my face."

There is no compromise in this training. If you want Berkeley to stop, you must make him stop completely. There is no way to train him that it is okay to give you two or three licks, because he won't understand that there is a limit to the number of times he can lick. He will understand that he can't lick at all.

If Berkeley doesn't get the message after you have pushed him away several times, put him out of the room. You must be tough and consistent if you want to teach Berkeley nice bedtime manners. Try again tomorrow night and keep it up until Berkeley understands that you mean business.

Why this works By giving Berkeley the attention he wants through play and more attention and affection in nightly grooming sessions, you tell him clearly that he is important to you. Consistently pushing him away and giving verbal reinforcement to your demands will eventually let Berkeley know where the limits are set.

Preventative tips Discourage unwanted behavior the first time and every time it happens. Remember that what is cute in a kitten may be unacceptable in an adult cat.

Licking plastic bags

Terra appears to be addicted to plastic bags. She will steal any plastic bag she can get her teeth on: sandwich bags, clear produce bags, or plastic grocery bags. She will drag the bag off and lick it as though it tastes good. She also will lie on the bags if we let her. Is there anything in the plastic that could hurt Terra? How can we make her leave the bags alone?

Why is my cat doing this? The attraction that plastic bags hold for cats is a mystery that is curiously widespread. Many think cats are simply interested in the residual odor of foods contained in the bags, but further observation proved that cats would lick bags that had contained shoes, clothing, or hardware, and bags that had never been used, as readily as they would those that had contained food. Cats appear to be more strongly attracted to clear plastic and to white and light-colored bags and to be less interested in the dark green or black bags. They will avoid bags that have contained foods naturally repellent to cats, such as lemons and oranges.

The cat's sense of smell is believed to be even more highly developed than that of dogs, which is far more powerful than that of humans. Because the attraction to plastic bags is so widespread among cats, possibly there is some faint odor, completely undetectable by the puny human olfactory organ, that cats find enticing. Or perhaps cats enjoy the slick, cool texture of the plastic bags on their tongues.

And it is this texture of the plastic bags that may induce cats to lie on them. While cats tolerate and even seek out heat sources, they do occasionally get uncomfortably warm, and on initial contact a plastic bag is a cool surface to lie on.

How can I make her stop? Plastic bags should be kept out of the reach of children and cats. While the superthin bags such as those used to protect dry cleaning are the most dangerous, even heavier bags are dangerous for children and pets. It is possible for a child or pet to suffocate if a piece of plastic becomes stuck over their nose and mouth. Smaller pieces of plastic can easily be sucked into the windpipe and cut off the oxygen supply. (Another plastic item that is dangerously attractive to cats is the plastic ring set from six-packs of juice or soft drinks. These also need to be kept out of reach of small hands and paws.)

It might be possible to use taste-aversion therapy, such as dipping all your plastic bags in lemon juice, to convince Terra to leave them alone, or noise therapy to convince her that plastic bags are monsters and should be avoided. A simpler solution is to put the bags in a drawer or closet where Terra can't reach them. Plastic bags come in so many varieties that teaching Terra to stay away from each type would be a very time-consuming project. It is much easier to deny her access.

What to say and do Plastic ring sets should be removed from the cans they carry and cut through with a knife or scissors until no circles remain.

Immediately upon emptying plastic bags, put them in a drawer or closet where Terra can't get them. If the bags are going to be recycled, store them well out of reach; if they are going to be thrown away, tie them in knots and put them in the garbage.

Why this works The practical solution is to store the bags where Terra can't see them. Plastic bags are only casually attractive, not something that is so delectable that Terra will beat down a door to get at it after it has been put away. Plastic bags are an attraction that falls into the category of things that are out of sight, out of mind.

Preventative tips Keep plastic bags and plastic ring sets from cans strictly out of your cat's reach.

Licking self

Dancer licks himself all the time. He has licked all the fur off his backside and the backs of his legs and he just looks awful. He doesn't scratch or bite at the area, so I don't think he is doing it because he is itching. How can I make him stop and give his beautiful fur a chance to grow back?

Why is my cat doing this? Animals that are under a lot of stress sometimes lick or bite at themselves in an effort to ease the tension. This is called displacement activity. When they have licked so much that they are making themselves bald in spots, it is called displacement alopecia.

How can I make him stop? Sometimes cats engage in activities that appear bizarre in order to draw our attention to a situation we are unaware of. Take Dancer to your veterinarian for a complete physical examination to find out if there is a medical reason for his problem. If there is no medical reason for Dancer's licking, do a little detective work to learn the cause of his anxiety. Once you have eliminated the cause of the stress, Dancer should stop licking himself and allow his coat to blossom.

What to say and do If Dancer has not been neutered, consider having that done now. One of the most common causes of displacement alopecia is sexual frustration.

Overcrowding—a matter of too many cats in an area—can be very stressful to a sensitive cat, and sometimes one cat becomes the pariah. Watch the interaction among all your cats. Does Dancer spend most of his time up on a piece of furniture in an out-of-the-way area of the house? He may be the low man on the totem pole, and the other cats may not allow him free range of the house. If this is the case, consider separating Dancer with his own food, water, and litter box in a room where the other cats can't torment him. Other causes of Dancer's stress might be a toddler who chases him every time he gets off his perch or a dog that gives him much more attention than he desires.

Construction, barking dogs, and busy streets can make more noise than some cats are comfortable with. If your neighborhood is noisy during the day, leave a radio tuned to an easy-listening station to block out some of the clamor.

Exercise is one of the best ways to release pent-up tension, both for humans and animals. Make sure Dancer has a sturdy scratching post where he can work off his frustration and engage him in play. Some cats will not play, no matter how exciting the toy, if they have to compete with the other cats. Take Dancer into another room or put all the other cats out and spend a few minutes every day tossing the ball for him or dragging a toy on a string for him to chase. The kitty tease and the new toy that looks like a bird on a string, available in many pet stores, are ideal toys to get even the most lethargic or jaded cat moving. Few cats can resist when you are flicking one of these toys that mimic the movements of insects or birds. After the play session, spend a few minutes petting or grooming Dancer to give him a little extra attention and affection.

Why this works A buildup of tension has to go someplace. It expresses itself in medical problems, such as stomach ulcers or angry outbursts in humans and in excessive grooming in cats. Eliminating the cause of the stress and/or using extra attention and exercise to release it gives positive relief, and the problem ceases.

Preventative tips Resist bringing in more cats than you can comfortably feed, house, and play with. Make sure that all your cats have a little individual attention every day and that they are all getting some exercise. Teach children and puppies not to give the cats more attention than they can stand.

Licking stamps and envelopes

Sprite likes to lick and chew postage stamps and envelopes. At bill-paying time he is a real nuisance, walking all over the papers I'm working on and trying to lick everything. Sometimes he also licks and chews on photographs. Can these things make him sick? What does he find so stimulating about stamps and envelopes? How can I make him stop destroying my photographs?

Why is my cat doing this? Some adhesives are made from rendered animal components. Cats, with their exquisitely sensitive noses, are able to detect the most minuscule trace of a substance they find interesting in a compound that we find completely odorless and tasteless, such as the glue on a postage stamp.

The glue on postage stamps and envelopes does not appear to be detrimental to cats. It is unlikely that Sprite could ingest enough to cause himself any harm. However, Sprite's sharp teeth and wet little tongue can quickly destroy a fair amount of expensive postage and stationery.

Photographs go through a number of processes using chemicals that are certainly not designed to do a cat any good. Again, it is not likely Sprite would ingest enough of any of these chemical substances to cause harm, but he can destroy photographs that you value by removing the finish with his tongue and poking holes in them with his teeth.

Cats also often eat or lick substances that we would not expect them to find appealing, such as dirt, particles of concrete, chalk, or cat litter. Often these cats are well fed, content, and in apparent excellent health, as Sprite appears to be, so it is unlikely that he is licking and chewing your stamps, envelopes, and photographs for any reason other than that they taste interesting to him.

How can I make him stop? Postage stamps and stationery are not so attractive that Sprite will fight to get at them. Just put them in a drawer when you aren't using them. Train him to stay off your desk while you are working. Put him on the floor and offer a toy for him to play with or shut him out of the room to avoid his interference.

What to say and do When Sprite jumps onto the desk, use a *sharp clap* and say sternly, "Get off, Sprite. You aren't allowed on my desk." If Sprite doesn't jump down, pick him up and set him on the floor. Say, "No, Sprite. I'm trying to pay the bills and you are being a pest. Go find something else to do."

It is helpful to have a distraction, such as a jingle ball or a crumpled piece of paper you can toss for him to chase. Shake the ball or rub the wad of paper so it makes noise before you throw it. Say, "Here, Sprite, get the ball, go get it, Sprite," and toss the ball or paper so it bounces invitingly.

Continue to use the sharp clap or push Sprite off the desk every time he jumps up and continue telling him that he is not welcome to interfere with your work. If Sprite has always been allowed on the desk in the past, it will take repeated effort to teach him that he must stay down. Be firm and insistent.

If Sprite persists in jumping back on the desk every time you put him down, carry him out of the room and shut the door. Say, "You are not allowed on my desk, Sprite. If you won't stay off, you will have to stay out."

Why this works Cats learn to stop doing things that annoy us only after having the lesson repeated numerous times. The top of your desk offers many attractions that are fun to play with, so using a toy that makes an interesting noise helps to distract him.

Preventative tips It is easiest to train cats to do what you want before they develop bad habits. If you don't want your work interrupted by the cat walking across your papers, put him down the first time—and every time—he jumps up.

Litter box, never used

Our kitten was raised outside and never learned to use a litter box. He goes to the bathroom on the carpet. If he won't use the litter box, he will have to live outdoors. How can I get him to use the litter box?

Why is my cat doing this? Cats are fastidious creatures who want to hide evidence of their presence from possible predators and potential prey. They carefully bury their feces so its odor can't be detected. Often, cats who are brought indoors for the first time after they are adults will locate and use the litter box without any prompting because it offers the best material for covering their stool. Kittens usually start using the litter box between the ages of three and five weeks. If Frosty is not making any attempt to find a place where he can dig, he may have been taken away from his mother before he learned this behavior.

How can I make him stop? Frosty isn't being naughty on purpose—he just has yet to experience the pleasure of using a nice clean litter box. It should be relatively easy to show him where you want him to go to the bathroom, and once he learns he will continue to use the litter box.

What to say and do Young kittens defecate within a few minutes of eating. Select a litter box with fairly low sides so Frosty can scramble in and out without assistance. Place the litter box near where you feed him—don't put it right next to his food and water, but have it handy (five to ten feet is a good distance for youngsters). Immediately after he finishes eating his next meal, pick him up and place him in the litter box. The feel of the loose material should trigger Frosty's instinct to dig, but you may need to demonstrate by scratching the litter with your finger. Gently scratch the litter with his paw to show him what you expect. Don't squeeze and don't hold on if he tries to pull away. You don't want anything unpleasant to happen while he is in the litter box. Don't force Frosty to stay in the litter box, but keep a very close eye on him. He is going to have a bowel movement within the next few minutes. When you observe him making scratching motions or starting to squat, quickly scoop him up and place him in the litter box. Say in a light, cheerful voice, "Here, Frosty. This nice box is where you go to the bathroom."

Frosty may dig a little, or he may simply squat and do his business. If he doesn't cover his feces when he is finished, gently turn him so he can see what you are doing and use your fingers to cover it. Say, "There, all done. What a clever little cat you are, Frosty." Allow Frosty to climb out of the box by himself and go where he wants. Kittens can always find their way back to the litter box if they are allowed to walk away, rather than being carried.

Bear in mind that Frosty's little legs are very short, and the urge to urinate or defecate is followed quickly by the act. Make sure Frosty knows where there are litter boxes he can reach within a few seconds. Take him to each box in turn and place him in it, allowing him to leave when he wants. Even if he didn't need to use the box when you put him in it, he will remember where it is.

Many kittens learn to use the litter box after being placed in it one time, others take several tries, but all are surprisingly quick to catch on.

Why this works Frosty's instincts work in your favor. Cats don't like to leave their feces unburied. Frosty wants loose material to dig in and cover with, and the litter-box filler is ideal for this purpose.

Preventative tips Place kittens in the litter box first thing when you take them to a new home. Watch new kittens closely for the first few feedings to make sure they are using their box.

Litter-box filler (litter), scattering and tracking

We have a litter-box problem, but not the usual one. The problem is that our cat acts like he is digging his way to China. He digs with such zeal that litter flies out of the box in all directions and gets tracked all over the house. Sometimes he gets so carried away with his activities that he turns the box up on its side and dumps half the litter on the floor.

Why is my cat doing this? One of the reasons it is so easy to convince cats to use a litter box is that they want to bury their feces so predators won't find it and know there is a cat in the vicinity. Fagan is just doing an especially good job, making a nice deep hole to ensure adequate coverage. And while Fagan hasn't actually seen a coyote or wolf in your house, he sees no harm in being careful.

How can I make him stop? Fagan's litter box may be a little too small for him. Fagan needs to be able to turn around several times during his burying ritual so he can cover his feces from all directions. If the litter box is too small, he will be forced to step up on the rim of the box during one of these turns, and the contents then spill onto the floor. I have never had any success in making a devoted digger any less enthusiastic about the chore. Some cats are just dedicated diggers and will continue scratching away at the litter and the sides of the box long after they have buried the evidence. However, you can drastically reduce the amount of litter that gets scattered during Fagan's excavations.

What to say and do Try giving him a larger litter box (half again as long as he is). This larger box should also have higher sides, which will stop a lot of the scattering caused by his ardent digging.

An inexpensive solution to the scattering problem is to place Fagan's litter box inside a lidless cardboard box with one end cut out. The high sides on the cardboard box act to prevent the litter from being kicked out of the box onto the floor, while the open end allows Fagan easy access. Place a small rug in front of the opening to prevent Fagan from tracking the litter that is clinging to his feet.

There are several brands of covered litter boxes available in pet stores. These boxes are fully enclosed, with an opening in one end for the cat to go in and out. The box and cover are actually two pieces that can be taken apart for cleaning. However, you are going to have to be vigilant in preventing the covered litter box from becoming unattractive to Fagan. Because the box is covered, it is easy to neglect it.

Covered litter boxes are marketed as a device to eliminate the cat box odor from your home; some come with a filter for this purpose. Because they are covered, they do keep the odors pretty well confined inside the box. And that is the problem. If you can't see that the box needs cleaning, and it doesn't smell bad to you, you might forget to clean it—and poor Fagan will be the one to suffer.

Make sure the box is kept clean. Generally, you simply need to form the habit of checking the litter box twice a day to make sure it is clean and inviting, so Fagan won't need to find a less smelly place to use for his toilet.

Why this works Extra-tall sides, or complete covers, prevent your cat from throwing the litter out of the box in all directions. A small carpet placed in front of the opening will help remove any pieces of litter that cling to his feet as he leaves the box.

Preventative tips Make sure the litter box is large enough to allow Fagan to turn completely around. And make sure to keep it clean so Fagan will continue his good toilet habits.

See also:
Appendix (Litter-Box Care)

Litter-box odor

My cat's litter box smells terrible. I have to keep Cricket indoors because I live in a high-rise apartment and there is no way to allow her to go outside. I have tried several brands of litter, but nothing seems to make any difference. I even got a covered litter box with a filter in it, but that helps only part of the time.

Why is my cat doing this? Some foods and some digestive conditions produce particularly offensive stools, and Cricket may also be passing some gas that adds to the odor when she moves her bowels. It may also be that the litter box needs to be cleaned more often. Since Cricket's nose is far more sensitive than yours, she may be in a hurry to get away from the bad odor and might not be covering her feces as carefully as she normally would.

How can I make her stop? Litter-box odor, or its absence, is entirely in your control. If excessively offensive bowel movements are the problem, that condition needs to be corrected. Otherwise, keeping the litter box as clean as you keep your own toilet will eliminate any odor. Covering the litter box does not remove the odor, but simply traps most of it, making the box a very unattractive place for Cricket to spend time. Unless you can solve the odor problem, Cricket may decide to find herself a more appealing toilet, such as the carpet under the dining room table.

What to say and do If the food you are feeding Cricket smells bad when you open the can, it probably is not going to be improved by its journey through her digestive system. A high-quality, nutritionally balanced cat food may cost a few cents more, but it will be more completely utilized and will produce a less offensive stool. After only a few days of eating a high-quality food, Cricket's system will become accustomed to the more readily available nutrients, and she will actually eat less of the top-quality food and get more nutrition from it.

Check Cricket's stool to see whether it is well formed and fairly dark brown in color. If the odor is coming from the feces itself, the stool may be very loose or watery and may contain streaks of blood or mucus. If this is the case, have your veterinarian examine Cricket to see whether she has a medical problem. Cricket may need medication to correct the condition, or your veterinarian may recommend a dietary approach to the problem. If the odor is not coming from the stool but is an ammonialike odor coming from the cat litter in the box, the box just needs to be cleaned. Regardless of what brand of litter you use, urine starts to break down in a few days and odor starts to build up. There is no deodorant that will prevent the odor from forming, nor will covering the box eliminate it, even with a lid with a charcoal filter. The only solution is to empty the used litter out of the box, rinse and dry the box, and start over with clean litter. Ideally, clay-type litters should be changed every three days, or a minimum of once a week. Even the clumping-type litter will eventually become contaminated with tiny particles of urine-soaked materials that failed to adhere.

Why this works There are two sources of litter-box odor. One comes from stool and the other from the chemical decomposition of urine. The only way to eliminate the odor is to discard the soiled litter, wash the box, and fill it with new litter.

Preventative tips Feed your cat the best-quality food you can afford. Scoop solids out of the litter box once or twice a day, and completely empty the box and wash it at least once a week.

Lying on heat sources

No matter how warm the room is, my cat wants to lie right on top of the heat vent. If I have the door closed to the other rooms, the room cools off because he is blocking the heat. Is there any danger from his becoming too hot? How can I keep him off the vent so the whole room will stay warm?

Why is my cat doing this? George is exhibiting common cat behavior. Cats seem to love the heat and will lie in windows with the sun beating down on them or on top of radiators and heat vents that are uncomfortably warm to our touch. Cats lie on radiators, heating pads, and other heat sources that are hot enough to damage their skin and coat. Too much concentrated heat will give George dry, flaky skin, and the warm air blowing from the vent will dry out his coat.

How can I make him stop? You can temporarily discourage George from lying on the heat vent by using the *magazine toss* or *spray bottle,* but the warmth is probably too attractive to allow you to truly break George from this habit. You can fix the vent so George is not blocking the warmth from the rest of the room and elevate him away from the vent, so he is not in direct contact with it.

What to say and do To get George to move off the vent so the rest of the room gets some heat, pick him up and carry him away. Say, "George, you are blocking the heat from the room and scorching your beautiful fur. Come sit over here for a while." You can also try to wake George up by playing with him with a jingle ball, a crumpled wad of paper that makes interesting noise when you crinkle it, or with a fishing pole–type toy. The kitty tease and feathered friend are available in pet stores or through magazine ads and are almost impossible for any cat to resist. Getting George to move around will at least allow some warm air to circulate in the rest of the room.

When George returns to the vent, use the magazine toss or spray bottle again. If you are close to George, use a *sharp clap* and say sternly, "George! You are hogging all the heat. Get off the vent!"

A more permanent solution is to place a plastic milk crate over the vent. These vented plastic boxes are available in hardware and houseware stores. Turn the crate upside down over the vent and place a folded towel or cloth place mat on top of it. George can still lie where he gets the heat he craves, but he is elevated by the carton and slightly insulated by the towel or place mat so his skin and coat won't suffer damage from the excess heat. He no longer blocks the heat from everyone else, since the grill-like sides of the crate allow the warm air to flow into the room.

Why this works Distracting George with toys and startling him with the magazine toss or spray bottle are just temporary cures. As soon as your attention is elsewhere, George will most likely return to his cozy vent. The upside-down milk carton is a compromise that will allow both of you to be warm.

Preventative tips Place a layer of insulation between your cat and any heat source. Space heaters should be turned off and unplugged when you aren't able to supervise.

Mats and tangles

I have a very pretty long-haired cat, but he keeps getting mats. When I try to remove them he bites me and runs away. Is there any way to keep Diego from getting mats, or to make him hold still so I can comb them out?

Why is my cat doing this? Diego, and all long-haired cats, may develop mats in their coats from time to time. Matting is more common in the spring when Diego is shedding his winter coat faster than he can remove the loose hair, but mats can occur at any time of year. If Diego is allowed outside, small bits of vegetation (such as grass seeds or burrs) or sticky substances (such as tar or sap from trees) may form the base for a mat to develop.

Diego may bite because it hurts when you pull on the mat and he may object to being restrained during this sometimes painful procedure. If Diego is badly matted, you might be well advised to take him to your veterinarian or to a professional groomer to have the mats removed.

Begin short, daily grooming sessions immediately after Diego comes home from his trip to the beauty shop. Short, gentle sessions with lots of companionable chatter telling Diego what a handsome fellow he is will keep his fur in tip-top shape.

If Diego's mats are few and small enough that you want to attempt to remove them yourself, buy a professional mat splitter at a pet store or a seam ripper from a fabric store. Both of these instruments are designed with a sharp edge to cut through the packed hair of a mat, with a protective tip to prevent you from stabbing Diego while you work. The other tool you need is a small stainless-steel comb, available from a pet store or from a groomer.

Place Diego on a countertop so you have both hands free. If it is necessary to restrain Diego, just circle him with your arm, or lay your hand gently on his shoulders or chest. Gently grasp his tail and run the comb through the fur on the end, combing in the same direction the hair grows and being careful not to pull. Croon to Diego while you work. Say, "Diego, you are going to look so smart when we get all these awful tangles out." When you encounter a tangle or mat, stop immediately. Grasp that section of hair close to Diego's skin, and hold it firmly, without pulling, and gently comb the hair that protrudes from your hand. If the mat is too solid to be worked out with the comb, gently insert the mat splitter and push it gently through the mat. It will take several passes with the splitter to break up all but the smallest of mats.

When Diego starts to object, stop and scratch his chin and ears with your hand. Say, "Oh, I'm sorry, I didn't mean to pull your hair." Stroke his throat, chin, and head with the comb until he relaxes, then once again start gently working on the mat.

Keep the sessions very short, use a light touch, and don't forget to praise Diego for being brave. Watch Diego's ears. If he lays them back, stop combing and return to scratching his chin and ears until he relaxes once more. Do a little every day or twice a day. At the end of the session, even one that lasted only thirty seconds, praise Diego for his patience. Say in a cheerful voice, "What a strong, brave, handsome fellow you are, Diego. Good job. Let's take a break and finish this later."

Why this works Having the proper tools, keeping the sessions short, avoiding pain, and praising Diego for his cooperation will prevent Diego's heading for the hills every time he sees the comb. With enough patience on your part he may even come to enjoy his grooming sessions.

Preventative tips Kittens should be introduced to the pleasures of being groomed long before they need it. Check Diego for vegetation or sticky matter in his fur when he comes indoors and remove any foreign matter immediately. Make daily combing or brushing a part of your way of showing Diego your affection for him.

Medicine, won't take

M y cat has a cold. The veterinarian sent some pills home with me, but my cat spits them out and scratches and bites when I try to give them to her. How can I get her to stop fighting me and take the pills so she will get better?

Why is my cat doing this? Blackberry doesn't like to be restrained; she doesn't want you to pry her mouth open, and she hates the taste of the pill. Forcing the issue makes her frantic, and she bites and scratches in an effort to escape.

How can I make her stop? Your distress at having to try to poke the pill down her reluctant throat contributes to Blackberry's distress. Try to be calm, cheerful, and matter-of-fact about the business—and expect her to cooperate.

What to say and do If the medication is a nice, firm little pill that has a hard coating, tuck the pill into a small amount of a treat that Blackberry adores, such as strained beef for babies, and let her lick it off your finger, or wrap it in a tiny amount of her favorite canned food and put it on her plate and let her eat it. This only works with pills that do not taste terrible or those that are coated or hard enough that they don't melt into the treat they are hidden in.

For larger or softer-textured pills, place Blackberry on the counter and lightly pin her hindquarters against your waist with your elbow. Make a V with the little finger and ring finger of the same hand. Turn your hand palm up and place the notch of the V formed by your fingers across the back of her neck. Turning your hand slightly sideways, reach over the top of her head and grasp and lift her upper jaw with your index finger and thumb, gently tilting her head back in the process. With the other hand, place the pill over the hump of her tongue, pushing it as far back as your finger will reach. Lower her head, relax your grip on her muzzle, and push her lower jaw closed, allowing her to swallow. You will know you were successful when Blackberry licks her nose. If Blackberry stoutly resists, wrap her in a bath towel so only her head protrudes and use the same procedure for opening her mouth and inserting the pill. The towel will prevent Blackberry from clawing you in her efforts to escape and will eliminate the task of trying to keep her in one spot long enough to pry her mouth open.

Talk to Blackberry during the procedure, praising her for being brave and telling her how good she is going to feel when the medicine makes her well. Be cheerful and positive. You are doing her a favor by trying to cure her cold. Say, "What a big, brave girl you are, Blackberry. What a smart cat to know how good the pills are for you. Oh, you are going to feel so much better when you have taken all the pills and gotten rid of this nasty cold."

If you find that you are not able to get Blackberry to take her medication no matter how hard you try, take her back to the veterinarian and have him demonstrate how to give her a pill. After all, the pills won't work if you can't get her to take them. Alternatively, you may find it easier to give a liquid medicine rather than a pill. Ask your veterinarian if Blackberry's medication is available in liquid form, or if the pills can be crushed and placed in a solution.

Why this works The combination of your elbow on Blackberry's hips and your forearm along the side of her body give Black-

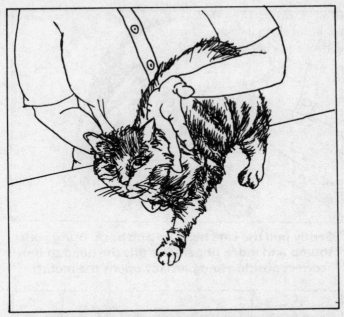

Make a V with your ring and pinkie fingers and place the V over the cat's neck, with your palm facing the cat's ears.

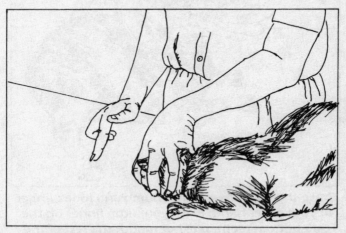

Reach over the cat's head, then gently but firmly grasp her upper jaw with your thumb and index finger.

Gently pull the cat's head up and back, using your thumb and index finger. This tilts the head to the correct position and partially opens the mouth.

Grasp the pill between the thumb and index finger of your other hand. Place your little finger on the cat's bottom teeth, pull her mouth the rest of the way open, and place the pill on the back of her tongue. Lower her head to allow her to swallow.

berry a feeling of being securely held without undue force. The "forked-stick" hold gives you a great deal of control in positioning Blackberry's head and keeping it still for the few seconds it takes to insert the pill over the back of her tongue, where it is very difficult for her to spit out.

Preventative tips When your cat is young, train her to allow you to open her mouth so medicating will be easily accomplished in the future.

Meowing, constant

Our cat has always been a lovely companion with no bad habits, but lately she has been meowing constantly and she is driving us crazy. What can we do to make her stop?

Why is my cat doing this? There are several possible explanations for Dolly's crying. She may, for example, have become an adult while you weren't looking. Cats reach sexual maturity as early as five months of age, and some display sexual behavior even earlier. If Dolly is sexually intact, she is most likely in estrus (in heat) and her meowing is an effort to attract a mate. She very likely is also spraying urine in an effort to attract a boyfriend.

Loss of her kittens, a loved person, or a companion pet might also cause Dolly to cry constantly; there is also a chance that she is in pain and needs medical attention.

How can I make her stop? If Dolly is not spayed and you do not plan for her to have kittens, take her to your veterinarian and have the surgery done. Your veterinarian will tell you that Dolly will live a longer, healthier life if she is spayed and kept indoors, and it will relieve her of the stress of being in heat.

Unless Dolly has recently suffered the loss of her kittens, a loved person. or a companion pet, take her to the veterinarian for a complete physical examination. There are many conditions that cause pain, and obviously Dolly is trying to communicate her need for help.

What to say and do If Dolly has experienced a loss and is grieving, the only remedy is your love and attention, and ultimately the passage of time. Spend extra time with Dolly, just as you would with a human friend who has lost a loved one. Extra grooming and petting sessions are in order. Croon to Dolly while you pet and groom her. Say, "Oh, Dolly, I know you are sad because your friend is gone. It is hard to lose friends, but you still have me, and I love you." Dolly loves being near you and the sound of your voice, so it doesn't matter much what you say, as long as your tone is soothing.

Use distraction to take Dolly's mind off her loss. This is a good time to buy her a few new toys or dig out the toys she hasn't played with for a while. Toss wadded-up paper, jingle balls, or Ping-Pong balls for her to chase, or drag a ribbon or toy across the floor. Put some energy and enthusiasm into these play sessions. A bright, cheerful tone will help divert her attention. Say, "Come on, Dolly, time to chase the ball. Go get the ball, Dolly." The game sessions are even more interesting if the toys make a little noise. Crinkle the paper or shake the ball to make it jingle before you toss it for her. The kitty tease or feathered friend makes an interesting sound as you flick it around, adding to the excitement.

With your help, Dolly should overcome the worst of her grief in a week or two. If she continues to cry in spite of your efforts, do have your veterinarian look for physical causes that might be contributing to her condition and ask him about the temporary use of medication to relieve her distress.

Why this works Extra attention, grooming, petting, and conversation will help distract your cat from what is bothering her and will make her feel more secure. Vigorous exercise helps release pent-up anxiety and recharges your cat's batteries so she has the energy to focus on the positive things in her life.

Preventative tips Have all your pets neutered as soon as your veterinarian says they are mature enough for the procedure. Always have your veterinarian examine your pets if there is a change in their behavior that you cannot explain.

Messy eater

I've heard that cats are very clean pets, but Amanda makes a real mess when she eats. She takes chunks of food out of her dish and carries them onto the carpet to eat. She also scatters her dry food all over the floor. Why is she so messy?

Why is my cat doing this? Amanda is following an instinct that would serve her well in the wild. Grabbing a chunk of food and moving a short distance away will allow her to eat without interference. Moving away from the food source would prevent other cats in a colony from swatting her to drive her away from a carcass or from taking her food away from her.

The spillage of dry food is caused by putting too much food on a flat plate. When the food is piled too high, normal movements during eating cause it to scatter. After the food has remained on the plate for several hours, it loses its appeal, and Amanda may be playing with it rather than eating it. Amanda would prefer having smaller servings of fresh food on a clean plate.

How can I make her stop? First be sure that Amanda is allowed to eat in peace, without interference from small children or other pets. She is hungry, but it is no fun to eat if you have to cope with a toddler trying to pick you up or a dog trying to steal your food. Make sure there are enough plates for all your cats so Amanda doesn't feel the need to snatch a mouthful and run with it. Also make sure that Amanda's feeding area is well out of the traffic lane so she doesn't have to worry about someone stepping on her while she is trying to eat.

What to say and do Find a place where Amanda won't be pestered by children, adults arriving home from work, or the dog. You may have to feed her on top of the washing machine, on the counter in the laundry room, or in the bathroom. Be sure to provide her with fresh water and don't shut her away from her litter box.

If you have more than one cat, give each cat a separate dish, spaced a foot or so apart. Cats generally examine each plate in turn, just to make sure there isn't something better in the next dish, but eventually they settle down to their own dish.

Place Amanda's dish on a serving tray to contain accidental spills. Hardware and houseware stores carry inexpensive plastic trays with raised edges that work well and are easy to sanitize between feedings. Use a shallow bowl to contain Amanda's dry food and don't pile it quite so high. If the dry food is being scattered around the room, she probably has more than she wants or needs.

If Amanda insists on carrying her canned food onto the carpet, cut it into bite-size pieces. She may still run and crouch on the carpet while she chews and swallows, but she will soon discover that this is not a very efficient way to eat and should eventually learn to eat at the designated spot.

Why this works Cats are really fairly tidy animals. Giving Amanda a peaceful place to eat will eliminate the need to scurry to a safe place with her food. A tray and a dish that hinders spillage will help keep the area neat.

Preventative tips Train your children and the dog to leave Amanda alone while she eats, or provide her with a place where they can't reach her. Allow Amanda a place where she feels safe, so she won't feel the need to hide in order to eat. Wash Amanda's dishes every day (or use paper plates and throw them away daily) and always provide fresh, clean drinking water.

Mounting

O ur five-month-old cat has started mounting all the other cats in the house. The girls are not in heat and they are all neutered, so he can't be trying to have sex with them. How can we make him stop this unattractive behavior?

Why is my cat doing this? Franklin may be experiencing the hormonal change that accompanies the onset of sexual maturity or he may be displaying territorial dominance. Males, particularly adolescents who have not yet figured out what is happening to their bodies, will frequently try to mate with females who are not in heat. They will mount neutered females, other male cats, and even young kittens. Five months is on the young side for a cat to reach sexual maturity, but it is by no means unheard of. The long, slender breeds, such as the Siamese and Oriental Shorthair, commonly enter puberty several months before their stockier-bodied counterparts do.

Territorial dominance mounting is a behavior that is common throughout the animal kingdom and is completely independent of any sexual urges. The dominant animal in a group will mount others to demonstrate his supremacy.

How can I make him stop? If Franklin's mounting behavior is sexual, neutering him will end his attempts to mate with the other cats in the household and will prevent him from spraying urine on walls and furniture to advertise his availability. It may take as long as two months for the hormones to completely leave his system, but the mounting should stop fairly quickly after his surgery.

What to say and do Ask your veterinarian about the possibility of Franklin's being sexually mature and whether he is old enough to be neutered.

Mounting can develop into a habitual activity that is not indicative of anything except the fact that Franklin is bored. Franklin can be discouraged from mounting other cats in the household by using the *magazine toss* or *spray bottle* or by giving a *sharp clap*. Use one of these tools and say sternly, "No, Franklin! Leave her alone!"

Spend ten or fifteen minutes every evening helping Franklin blow off some of his excess steam by playing an active game with him. Use the kitty tease or feathered friend (a fishing pole–type toy with a cloth or feather lure on a string) to get him moving. After a few minutes of dashing around the room and flying through the air, Franklin will probably be more socially acceptable company.

If Franklin is the dominant cat in the household, he may continue to mount the other cats periodically to display his superiority. Knowing that this is normal behavior may help you to accept it.

If you think Franklin is truly excessive in his mounting behavior, consult your veterinarian about medical intervention. There are drugs that will help eliminate mounting, but they should be used as a last resort. Give Franklin's system a chance to get rid of the hormones that are already in circulation, use play to help him cope with his pent-up energy or boredom, and give your training program a chance to work before you resort to chemicals.

Why this works Neutering ends the production of the hormones that are the major cause of mounting behavior. Vigorous play relieves boredom and provides an outlet for the extra energy young cats have in such abundance, and the shock of the *magazine toss* or *spray bottle* makes mounting an activity that has unpleasant results.

Preventative tips Engage your cats in vigorous play as a part of the daily routine to give them a healthful outlet for their energies. Have all your pets neutered as soon as your veterinarian says they are old enough—before they have a chance to develop sexually based bad habits.

Overly friendly, acting

My cat is overly friendly. She rubs around my ankles and meows until I pick her up and pet her. Every time I sit down she jumps into my lap and kneads and purrs and rubs her face all over mine. How can I make her behave like a normal cat?

Why is my cat doing this? Very few behavioral traits are breed specific (common only to one breed), but some breeds are inclined to be much more affectionate than others. Siamese, Balinese, and Oriental Shorthairs are breeds that are likely to be very loving toward their owners.

Cats who are left alone all day are more inclined to be overly affectionate when their people come home, and females of any breed, when in heat, can be aggressively friendly, rubbing the scent from glands near the base of their tail and near the corner of their mouth on their owners to mark their ownership of these special people.

How can I make her stop? A long-standing problem requires a long cure. Plan to spend a month or more teaching Jenny how you want to interact with her. Having Jenny spayed will stop behavior that is due to her being in heat, and a companion pet could keep her from getting too lonely while you are at work. You *can* set limits on how much and what sort of attention you will give and take.

What to say and do Unless you are planning to use Jenny in a breeding program, have her spayed. This will eliminate the cyclical, hormone-induced overly affectionate behavior.

It is normal for Jenny to be glad to see you, and to want your undivided attention, after being alone all day. Consider adding another cat to your household to keep Jenny company during the day and to absorb some of her zealous affection. A kitten will be easier to introduce than another adult cat, and in either case the introduction should be gentle.

Jenny should be given the same consideration you would give any member of your family. When you come home from work, spend a few minutes telling her about your day and asking about hers. Say, "Hello, Jenny. How are you this evening? Did you have a good day? Well, come tell me all about it." Invite Jenny to sit with you while you unwind from your day.

When Jenny starts to rub in your face, gently push her head away and say, "Don't do that, Jenny. I really don't like you to rub your face against mine." You must be consistent and firm. When you tire of pushing her away and telling her you don't like what she is doing, set her on the floor. Say, "Jenny, you can't sit in my lap if you insist on rubbing in my face. I don't like it when you do that." Get up and leave the area. Jenny will probably try to wind herself around your feet in an effort to get more attention from you. Don't fall for it. Say, "No, Jenny, I'm busy now. I don't have time to pick you up," and gently push her away with your foot. When your patience is exhausted, put her in another room and close the door. Say, "I'm sorry, Jenny, but you have to learn not to pester me when I'm busy."

Continue insisting that your relationship has to be on your terms, not hers. Jenny will eventually accept the change.

Why this works Cats generally get what they want by being very insistent. You have to be just a little more stubborn in order to get what you want. Consistently pushing her away will eventually convince her to stop rubbing your face.

Preventative tips Correct unwanted behavior the first time and every time it happens. It is too much to expect Jenny to understand that it is okay to rub in your face sometimes, but not okay at other times. Make her stop every time.

See also:
Jealousy

Overweight

Our veterinarian says Monty is fat. He should weigh about eight pounds, but he is closer to twelve. He has been on a diet for over a month, but he isn't losing weight. How can we make him stop eating so much?

Why is my cat doing this? Like people, some cats eat anything and everything they want and still manage to stay fashionably trim. Others try everything to lose weight and still remain heavy. Some cats seem convinced that famine is just over the horizon and feel compelled to eat as much as possible. Others nibble daintily at whatever food is offered, and some cats are too busy to be bothered to eat more than is absolutely necessary to sustain them. Boredom and lack of exercise combine to keep Monty plumper than he should be.

How can I make him stop? Brace yourself to do what must be done to help Monty regain his waistline. You must take complete control of Monty's diet and exercise program and see to it that he has the right combination of diet and exercise to trim off those excess pounds.

What to say and do Your veterinarian has no doubt offered you a selection of programs to help Monty lose weight. Some veterinarians recommend feeding your cat a food formulated especially to prevent weight gain in less active cats, or one designed to help the cat reduce. Still others recommend keeping the cat on his regular diet but reducing the amount offered. Your veterinarian is best trained to determine which cat food formula is best for Monty's age and condition. Follow his advice about what Monty should eat and how much he should be offered. Use a measuring cup to keep yourself honest about the amount of food you are giving Monty and turn a deaf ear to his pitiful pleas for more. Be sure to follow your veterinarian's instructions exactly. Reducing Monty's weight too quickly could result in a liver condition called hepatic lipidosis.

Prevent Monty from having access to food other than what his veterinarian has recommended by confining him to the house or to his outside run. If you have been faithful in following your veterinarian's instructions and are not seeing results, Monty probably has another source of food. He may be a successful hunter, catching birds and mice to supplement his diet, or he may be an accomplished mooch, canvassing the neighborhood in search of handouts. Monty may have a regular route he follows, cadging tidbits or whole meals from unsuspecting neighbors who think he is a stray in need of sustenance.

Exercise is an important part of any weight-loss program. Monty won't think about food while he is chasing a kitty tease or feathered friend or fetching a ball or wad of paper, and playing with him will entertain you, too. Adding a few minutes of exercise to Monty's day will help run off some of the fat and, the experts say, raise his metabolism somewhat.

Why this works Cats become overweight when they consume more calories than they burn. Restricting Monty's intake of food, while increasing his activities so he uses more energy, will alter that balance in favor of weight reduction.

Preventative tips Feed your cat a diet prepared especially for his or her age and adjust the amount at the first sign your adult cat is getting pudgy. Kittens should not be put on a diet except under veterinary supervision. Restrict treats to small amounts of healthful foods and make sure your cats and kittens get plenty of exercise by playing with them.

Petting, always needs

Moose is a real pest. When he decides he wants to be petted, he meows, rubs around my ankles, butts me with his head, and pats my thighs with his paws until I pick him up and pet him. He seems to want me to scratch his head and jowls and meows and butts my hand until I do it right. My veterinarian said there is no evidence of any sort of parasite, and his skin seems in good condition. How can I make him behave like a normal cat so I can get my work done?

Why is my cat doing this? Perhaps Moose senses that you need to take a break, and his pet-me insistence is an effort to help you stop what you are doing for a moment and focus on something else. Cats can be surprisingly sensitive to your moods and quite creative in helping you relieve your tension.

Maybe Moose just wants his back scratched. Cats are as individual as people. There are cats who are content with a couple of strokes or a quick scratch behind the ears or under the chin and some who can't seem to get enough of your touch. Some cats want to be right up in your face, while others would prefer to lie beside you, rather than in your lap. Some cats like a very light stroke and some seem to enjoy vigorous scratching or a firm, massagelike touch.

How can I make him stop? Give Moose what he wants—a good petting—but do it on your terms. There is no reason to allow him to have his way all the time.

What to say and do Have you been sitting in one spot so long that your feet are going to sleep? Have you been wrestling with a problem until you have a headache? Maybe you do need to take a break, get up and stretch, and focus on Moose for a few minutes. Take advantage of the interruption, carry Moose into the other room, and give him a thorough brushing, paying extra attention to the spots he most likes to have scratched. Say, "You're right, Moose, I did need a break. How about a good brushing?" When his time is up, set him off your lap. Say, "There you go, Moose, all spruced up. Now I have to go back to work." Be firm about the amount of time you can spend taking a break. If Moose isn't willing to stop when you are, close the door to the work room, or put him in another room and close the door. Say, "No, Moose. I have to get some work done. We'll spend some more time together later."

If you don't want Moose to interrupt you when you are working, push him away when he starts pestering you. Say, "Not now, Moose, I'm busy," and give him a gentle shove. Continue pushing him away and telling him no until he stops pestering you. If he is too insistent, carry him out of the room and close the door. Say, "Not now, Moose, I'm busy. If you can't watch quietly, you'll have to go out." This will not work if you pet him some of the time and push him away at other times.

Have a regular grooming/petting session that Moose can count on. A few minutes a day spent brushing Moose will rid him of loose hair and flakes of dead skin and make him feel loved while strengthening the bond between you.

Why this works If Moose knows that he can look forward to having your undivided attention at his evening grooming session, he will be less inclined to interrupt your work. Putting him out of the room when he pesters you lets him know that his behavior is not wanted.

Preventative tips Schedule a regular time for relaxing and grooming Moose. Don't ever allow him to interrupt you when you are working unless you are willing to take periodic breaks.

Pouting

You are going to think I'm crazy, but I swear my cat is pouting at me. On normal workdays or when I go out for a few hours, Shawna greets me at the door, rubs around my ankles, and chirps to be picked up and loved. But when I come back from a business trip, I'm greeted by a totally different cat. She turns her back to me, sticks her nose in the air, and sniffs, as if to say, "Humph! Who needs you?" I can't give up my promotion just because my cat has her nose out of joint. On the other hand, I don't like having her give me the cold shoulder every time I have to take a business trip. How can I make her stop pouting?

Why is my cat doing this? You hit the nail right on the head. Shawna is indeed pouting at you for leaving her alone day after day, when you used to be home every night. Many cats sulk at their owners when they feel they are being abandoned or ignored. Some are so upset at what they perceive as abandonment that they express their disgust by urinating or defecating in the suitcase or on the clothes during packing or unpacking.

How can I make her stop? You need to let Shawna know that she isn't being abandoned and that she is an important part of your life. Even if you don't believe Shawna can understand what you say to her, talk things over with her. Certainly she understands a caring tone of voice.

What to say and do You may feel a little silly the first few times you try this technique, but you'll get over it when you see the results. Tell Shawna about your new position and how much you like it, in spite of the fact that you have to be gone from home from time to time. Tell her when you are going out of town and when you will be back. A few days before you leave, show her the calendar and say, "Shawna, I'm going to Chicago for three days. I'll be back this day, Thursday. You are in charge. Linda will be by twice a day to feed you and make sure everything is under control while I'm gone." The day of your trip, don't forget to say good-bye to Shawna. Say, "Good-bye, Shawna. See you Thursday. Guard the house." You may feel silly sharing your travel plans with a cat, but Shawna's improved attitude will make it worth the embarrassment.

Homecoming is a time for treats and extra attention. Make a fuss over Shawna when you come in. Say in your most cheerful voice, "Hi, Shawna, I see the house is still standing, and you are looking exceptionally attractive. It sure is good to be home!" Give her some of her favorite treat (most cats adore baby foods such as strained beef or chicken) and say, "You did a good job of taking care of the house while I was gone." Babble away. It doesn't matter what you say, as long as Shawna knows she has your undivided attention. This is also a good time to get out the kitty tease or jingle balls and spend a little one-on-one playtime.

Why this works Many people don't believe that cats understand English or that they know one day from the next. But the experience of many cat lovers is that cats understand—if not the words—your tone, your body language, and the fact that they have your undivided attention. Some people believe that cats are waiting in their greeting spot when travelers return because they recognized the sound of the car, but spouses report that several minutes before the traveler's arrival, the cat stationed itself in the greeting spot, which had not been visited at all during the trip. We don't know why it works—it just does.

Preventative tips Treat your cat with the same regard you would give your child. Tell her when you are leaving and when you will return. All family members deserve this courtesy.

Quarrelsomeness

Joy is a lovely, sweet-natured cat when there is no other cat in the room, but she doesn't get along with our other two. The other two cats get along well together and they act like they want to be friends with Joy. We would like to have three cats and we thought Joy might like to have company while we are at work, but all she wants to do is argue. She lays her ears back and growls when we bring them into the room where she is. Is there any way we can get her to stop quarreling with the other cats?

Why is my cat doing this? Joy might very well enjoy the company of another cat, or several other cats, but she doesn't want her territory invaded and she may be a little worried that she will no longer be the center of attention. The fact that the other two cats are already friends may make it seem to Joy that they are ganging up on her.

The fact that Joy is just grumbling at the other two cats instead of attacking them makes it appear possible that she will accept them if given a proper introduction.

How can I make her stop? Separate Joy and the other two cats and reintroduce them slowly and gradually. Extra attention in the form of playtime, petting, and grooming, along with soothing words, will help Joy feel more secure and less compelled to defend her territory.

What to say and do For the moment, put the two new cats in another room and allow Joy to become accustomed to their scent without having direct confrontations. Visit the new cats in their room, but don't bring them into Joy's presence until she gets used to having them in the house.

Exchange sleeping equipment between the cats, putting the new cats' bedding in Joy's bed and her bedding in theirs. Even though you can detect no odor from either set of bedding, the cats' sensitive noses will detect a clear and probably powerful scent on the cloth.

Allow Joy to visit the other cats through the closed door. Leave her alone and allow her to growl at them if she seems to feel that is necessary. It is all right for her to let the newcomers know that she is top cat around here.

Give Joy a lot of extra attention and tell her about the new cats. While you are grooming her, say, "Joy, we got two new kitties to keep you company while we are at work. They are very nice cats, and we hope you are going to like them. Of course, you will still be our most important cat."

When Joy stops growling at the new cats through the door, start introductions. Take Joy on your lap and stroke her while an assistant sits across the room petting and talking gently to one of the other cats. If Joy is calm, allow her to take a closer look at the cat if she wants. Have a kitty tease or feathered-friend toy ready to use as a distraction in case Joy decides to start an argument. If Joy starts growling, dangle the lure in front of her and say, "Come on, Joy, let's get the bird. Never mind that cat, she doesn't have anything to do with you." If Joy won't be distracted by a toy, pick her up and say, "I guess it is a little too soon for introductions, isn't it? We'll try again later." Have your assistant take the new cat back to her quarters.

Several days of petting Joy in the presence of one of the other cats should help her relax and accept them.

Why this works When cats are left to their own devices, they live together in colonies. They may not be the best of friends, but they learn to tolerate one another. If you are relaxed and confident and Joy doesn't feel too pressured, she should accept some company.

Preventative tips Introduce new pets gradually, making sure the resident cats gets extra attention to prevent jealousy.

See also:
Jealousy

Roaming

Our cat won't stay home. He roams around the neighborhood during the day and is sometimes gone all night. Once or twice he has disappeared for as long as three days. We worry about him when he doesn't come home. How can we make him stay in the yard?

Why is my cat doing this? Cats who are allowed outdoors have a territory of several blocks that they travel in a fairly routine fashion, usually arriving back home in time for dinner. You are right to be concerned about Lance's roving. It is likely that he doesn't come home some nights because he is cowering under a porch or clinging to a tree limb, waiting for a ferocious dog to go away. Perhaps Lance doesn't come home some nights because he is hanging around a neighbor's house, trying to find a way to get in to see a female that is in heat. There is always the possibility that one night Lance will not come home because statistics have finally caught up with him and he has been hit by a car.

How can I make him stop? The only way to be sure Lance will be safely at home in the evening is to stop allowing him to go outside. An alternative to allowing him to roam at will is to build an open-air enclosure with access through a cat door or a window.

What to say and do An outside run need not be large or elaborate—even a small structure can give him the feeling of being outside. Consider screening in a patio or porch (or check the advertisements in cat-related magazines for ready-built enclosures) to provide Lance with fresh air, sunshine, and a fairly unobstructed view of the world, while preventing him from annoying the neighbors and keeping him out of harm's way. An enclosure constructed from boards and chicken wire or hardware cloth can be designed to fit any space you have available. If the enclosure is large enough, furnish it for him with something to scratch, something to climb, and shelves at various levels where he can perch, and place one or two litter boxes in the run to complete the sense that he is really out of the house. Make sure Lance can get out of the weather, either back into the house through a window or cat door or into a shelter, and that he has access to fresh water.

If you feel you can't provide an outside enclosure for Lance, make sure he has a good, sturdy scratching post where he can exercise his claws. The scratching post should be large enough so he can stretch full length and sturdy enough that it won't topple over when he tries to use it.

Spend a little extra time playing with Lance to help him burn off some of his excess energy. The kitty tease and the feathered friend (toys composed of a piece of cloth or feathers attached to a wand) are both irresistible to cats. Lance might also enjoy chasing a jingle ball, or even a crumpled wad of paper.

Why this works Many cats like to roam the neighborhood pretending to be lord of the jungle, but thousands of cats live long, healthy, happy lives without ever going outside. Giving Lance an enclosure that allows him to go outside without really being outside will help to keep him from feeling too confined. Cats who are neutered do not suffer from the biological drive to mate and are much less eager to explore.

Preventative tips Keep your kitten indoors. If he has never been outside, he will not know he is missing anything. To prevent the urge to roam that is caused by the desire to mate, have your kitten neutered as soon as your veterinarian says he is old enough.

Runaway (lost in transit)

The last time we moved, we lost our cat. After the moving van left, we discovered the cat was missing. We looked all through the house, in every closet and cupboard, and combed the neighborhood for hours, but he was nowhere to be found. Finally, it got so late we had to leave without him. A few days later one of our old neighbors called and said Caesar was on her back porch looking for food, and we were able to go back and get him. We are moving again, this time across the country. If Caesar disappears again, we won't be able to get him back by just driving across town. How can we keep Caesar from running away?

Why is my cat doing this? Cats are notorious for their dislike of change and their distaste for commotion. The excitement caused by the arrival of the moving van, the strangers in the house, and all the packing going on probably upset Caesar. In the midst of the confusion, Caesar took advantage of an open door and escaped from the uproar. Using a survival technique that has served cats well over the centuries, Caesar found a protected hiding place and stayed there until he thought it was safe to emerge. You may have walked right by him in your search, but he was still too frightened at that time to come out.

How can I make him stop? You can train Caesar to come or answer when called. With the proper inducement, Caesar will respond to your voice or your signal even if he is frightened. Training him to come when called will help you locate him if he disappears again, but it is more important to keep him where you can find him when you are ready to go.

What to say and do Early on moving day, before the confusion starts, confine Caesar to one room in the house and put a big "Do Not Open This Door!" sign on the door. Tell everybody who is helping with the packing that Caesar is in that room and that they are not to open the door under any circumstances. Put Caesar's carrier, his bed, food and water dishes, and litter box in the room with him, along with any other items he will need during the trip to the new home. When it is time to go, all you have to do is put Caesar in his carrier and ferry him and his equipment out to the car.

Keep Caesar in his carrier while traveling. The carrier serves the same purpose as a child's car seat during travel—it protects Caesar in case of accident, and it prevents him from interfering with the driver. Keeping Caesar in his carrier will also keep him from jumping out of the car and becoming lost in a strange area. If you have to stay overnight in a motel, be sure to put Caesar in the bathroom or confine him to his carrier while you are moving in and out of the room.

Keep Caesar indoors in your new home for at least three weeks, until he knows this is his home. Cats become very attached to their old homes and neighborhoods and it is common for them to try to return to their old home.

Why this works Far from being cruel, you are being kind to Caesar by confining him to a room and to his carrier so he won't get lost. Three weeks is the average length of time it takes for a new habit to develop—in this case, for Caesar to become accustomed to his new home.

Preventative tips Train Caesar to come when called. There are many noisemakers, such as buzzers and clickers, that animal trainers use, but it is better to use a noise that you can make without any device.

Several times a day, for at least twenty-one days, call Caesar's name when he is out of your sight. When he comes, give him a tiny taste of his favorite treat. Reinforce the training by giving him his treat or a meal every time you call his name. Do not call him unless you are prepared to give him his treat. If you are faithful to this training program, he will come to you even if he is frightened.

"Scooting"

My cat sometimes "scoots" across the floor. He sticks his back feet straight out in front of him and drags his rear end across the rug. This obscene behavior is embarrassing—especially when we have company. Why is he doing this? How can I make him stop?

Why is my cat doing this? Do not ignore this behavior. Bentley is signaling you that he has a problem with his bottom. Scooting is a normal behavior in animals when their anal area is causing them some discomfort. Bentley may be trying to scrape off feces that got stuck in his fur when he had his last bowel movement or he may be experiencing pressure, burning, or itching in his anal area. Female cats with vaginitis or vaginal discomfort may also scoot.

How can I make him stop? You are going to have to discover what is causing Bentley's distress. If the problem is feces in his britches, you can most likely correct the situation. If not, you will need your veterinarian's help to relieve Bentley's discomfort. Roundworms or tapeworms can cause itching, and overfull anal glands (two small glands located on either side of the rectal opening) can cause a feeling of pressure and/or pain. These and other conditions can be very serious, and if Bentley doesn't have feces or other matter stuck on his bottom, your veterinarian should see him right away.

What to say and do Bentley is uncomfortable and needs soothing. Say, "Poor Bentley. Let's see what's wrong here," and pick him up to examine him.

First check to see if there is some stool stuck in the hair on his rear end. It may be pulling the hair and making him uncomfortable. If this is the problem, you need to help him clean the area. Using a tissue or toilet paper, remove as much stool as you can from the hair. Wash the fur with a warm, damp washcloth, or rub a little cornstarch into the hair to remove the last traces of feces. If Bentley still smells bad, you can remove the odor with a cloth dampened with Listerine. It is helpful to have a family member or friend distract Bentley while you clean his britches. Your helper should pet and scratch Bentley's head and chin, and both of you should talk sympathetically. Say, "Poor Bentley, we'll have this all cleaned up in just a minute. What a good kitty to stand so nicely to get cleaned up." Be extremely gentle and keep talking quietly while you work. It doesn't matter what you say as long as your tone is soothing. After his cleaning session, give him a little treat, such as a teaspoonful of strained beef or chicken to soothe his ruffled dignity.

If Bentley has excessive amounts of feces stuck in his fur or if the feces have dried, you may have to wash his fanny under running water or clip the affected hair away from the area. Be extremely careful with the scissors. Many an experienced groomer has accidentally clipped the cat instead of the mat. Adjust the temperature of the water so it is comfortable to your wrist—not too hot or too cool—before you put Bentley in the tub. A little dishwashing detergent will help remove the feces and eliminate the odor. Be sure to rinse thoroughly. It is important to remove fecal matter from Bentley's fur because it can cause the skin underneath to become sore and inflamed or infected if you ignore it.

If there are no feces on Bentley's behind, take him to your veterinarian for examination. Any of the problems that are causing Bentley to scoot could lead to serious conditions if left untreated.

Why this works Elimination of the physical discomfort that is causing Bentley to scoot will stop the behavior. Scooting is always an indication that your cat is experiencing pain or irritation to his rear end.

Preventative tips Make grooming your cat a part of your daily routine. Often minor problems are discovered during grooming sessions, preventing major problems later on.

See also:
Mats and tangles

Scratching the furniture

Our cat is destroying our couch. Several times a day she sharpens her claws on it. We are going to have to either have her claws removed or find her another home. She is a lovely cat and I don't want to lose her, but I want a nice home, too.

Why is my cat doing this? Tribble is behaving in a perfectly natural way, although she is using the wrong target to satisfy her needs. Sharpening their claws—or ridding themselves of the outer layer of old claw—is one reason cats claw, but not the only reason. Even declawed cats will continue to go through the motions of clawing (although, without their claws, they do not inflict any damage on the items they scratch) in order to mark their territory. There are scent glands in the paw pads, and this scent rubs off on the items they scratch. Once an item has been scratched by one cat, every other cat who comes within sniffing range will scratch the item in an effort to replace the strange scent with his own. Tribble may also get some mild exercise by stretching out and vigorously clawing the couch.

How can I make her stop? Tribble just needs a proper scratching post and a little gentle redirection for her energy. She has an inborn need to exercise her claws and will continue to scratch no matter what you do. However, if you provide her with an acceptable scratching post and discourage her from scratching the couch, you can stop her from destroying your furniture.

Get a scratching post that is tall enough for Tribble to stretch her full length and is sturdy enough that it will not fall over when she tries to use it. A fabric such as rope or sisal (the material that looks like carpet backing) offers a good, firm surface Tribble can really work out on. The very best posts are made by the Cat Tree Company in Seattle, Washington. The posts are not as pretty as those covered with carpet, but cats love them.

What to say and do If the fabric is not too delicate, use a commercial cat repellent or rub lemon or orange peel on the surfaces you don't want Tribble to scratch. Test any repellent in an unobtrusive spot to make sure it won't stain the fabric. Cover the spot with heavy plastic until Tribble begins using her official scratching post regularly.

Bring in the new scratching post and set it near the area Tribble has been scratching. Pick Tribble up and gently rub her paws on the post to impregnate it with her scent. Her scent on the post will encourage her to use it in the future. Put some excitement in your voice and say, "Oh, look, Tribble. We got you a new scratching post. Isn't it wonderful?" When Tribble approaches the couch to scratch, say, "No, no, Tribble, that's not the place to scratch." Place her on the post and say, "Here, Tribble, isn't this new post nice? This is where you sharpen your claws." Be gentle. The object is not to frighten or punish Tribble, but to redirect her. If she persists in trying to scratch the couch, inflate a lot of balloons and tape them to the spot she scratches. When she accidentally pops a balloon or two, she will be discouraged from scratching that piece of furniture. Also, use the *magazine toss* and *sharp clap* and say, "No, Tribble! Don't scratch the couch!"

Why this works Tribble needs to scratch almost as much as she needs to breathe. Most cats actually prefer a good scratching post to the furniture, and with a little gentle redirection will easily switch from one to the other.

Preventative tips Get a good, sturdy scratching post before you get a cat or kitten. Gently rub the cat's paws on the post as soon as she is over the trauma of traveling to her new home. If she scratches somewhere other than her scratching post, immediately take her over to the post and tell her this is where you want her to scratch.

Sitting on books and newspapers

I can't read a book or newspaper or balance my checkbook without Chipper getting in the middle of it. He seems to know exactly where to park himself in order to cause me the most annoyance. Why does he have to sit or lie on what I am trying to see? Is there any way to make him stop this annoying practice?

Why is my cat doing this? This behavior has never been satisfactorily explained. Cats seem to have an uncanny knack for knowing precisely which article you are trying to read or the particular column of figures you are trying to add. They unerringly place themselves where they can best obstruct your view.

One theory is that you are finally sitting quietly, and Chipper sees this as his opportunity to visit with you. Another idea is that Chipper senses that your checkbook won't balance and he is trying to distract you and give you a little break so you can return to your work refreshed. Another explanation is that Chipper is just being contrary and is enjoying your exasperation.

How can I make him stop? Use a combination of removing Chipper from your lap or desktop and a verbal display of displeasure to let him know that he is not welcome at this time. Chipper can be taught that it is okay to get in your lap when you are reading, but not okay to place himself between you and your article. If you do your reading in the same chair where you customarily give Chipper attention, you are going to have a very difficult time teaching him the difference between lying quietly on your lap and sitting with his head in front of your book, but he may eventually recognize the connection between the times you have a book or newspaper in your hands and the times you do not.

What to say and do Push Chipper's head out of your line of sight when he sticks it between you and your book. Say, "Down in front, Chipper, I can't see through you." When he sticks his head back in the way, push him down again and say, "Chipper, stay out of the way. I want to read now." Reward him for staying down by scratching his ears and chin while you read. If his head pops back into your line of vision, push it down again and use the *hiss*. Say sternly, "Stop it, Chipper! That is annoying!"

If he won't stay down, push him off your lap and say, "Get down! You can't sit on my lap if you won't behave yourself." When he tries to jump back up, use the hiss or the *sharp clap* and say sharply, "Stay down! I can't read with you in my face." If he continues to pester you, carry him out of the room and close the door. Say, "I can't read with you in my face. You'll have to stay out until you learn to behave."

When Chipper parks himself in the middle of your work, pick him up and place him on the floor. Say, "Not now, Chipper. I have to get the checkbook balanced." When he jumps back up, put him down again, and say firmly, "No, Chipper, I'm busy. I can't play right now." You can get Chipper to remove himself by using the sharp clap or the hiss to display your annoyance with him, but the slower route of continuing to lift him off your work and set him on the floor with a strong admonition to stay down is less likely to scatter your papers. If he won't stay down, carry him out of the room and close the door.

Why this works Chipper can be trained to stay off your desk the same way he is taught to stay off the table when you are eating. Consistently removing him, together with verbal reinforcement will eventually convince him that he is not welcome.

Preventative tips Be consistent. Don't allow him on your desk when you are in a good mood and make him stay off when you aren't.

Spraying, neutered female

My spayed female has recently started backing up to the wall and spraying urine. I thought only tomcats did this. How can I make her stop?

Why is my cat doing this? It is natural for both male and female cats to mark their territory. Since your cat is neutered, she is probably defending her territory against a new pet, a new family member or visitors, or a stray hanging around outside. For your cat to stop spraying, she has to be sure that her position in the household is secure.

What to say and do If you catch her in the act, say, "No, Betsy!" sharply, and use the *sharp clap* or *magazine toss*. This will stop the incident. If she hasn't run too far, pick her up gently and carry her to her litter box. Do not discipline your cat any further—punishment will only confuse her.

Wet a rag or sponge with plain water and wipe down the area where your cat has sprayed. Treat the area with a commercial odor remover to discourage her from repeating the act. Taping a big piece of aluminum foil over the spot will act as a deterrent—the noise of urine hitting the foil is objectionable to most cats. If she persists, place a dish of her food directly in front of the spot or place several strips of double-faced masking tape on the floor. Cats don't like to urinate around their food and they do not like having their feet stick to the floor.

Determine the cause of the problem. If there are no new people or pets living in your house, check the outside bottom of entry doors and window frames to see if a stray has sprayed.

If the problem is caused by extra people living in your home, put Betsy in a quiet room with her food, water, and litter box for a few days. Reassure her in a happy tone that you want her to be comfortable. "There, Betsy, maybe you need a little more privacy. It will be nice and quiet in here."

If the problem is caused by a new pet in the household, put your new pet in another room for a few days. Avoid making too much of a fuss over the new pet until your cat gets used to the idea of sharing her space. Provide an extra litter box. Betsy might not like the idea of sharing a toilet with this stranger.

In either case, give your cat extra attention for a few days until she accepts the additional family member. Take a few minutes to sit and *groom* her. Speak soothingly, saying, "I love you, Betsy. You are my special best friend cat. You are such a pretty girl. What nice fur you have." Be sincere. Even if you don't think she can understand the words you say, your voice will convey your love and reassure her that she is an important member of the household.

If Betsy persists in spite of your efforts, consult your veterinarian about chemical intervention. Ovaban—a birth-control pill for dogs—has been used successfully to control spraying, but it does have side effects. Ask your veterinarian about newer drugs with fewer drawbacks.

Why this works Betsy is spraying because her territory has been invaded. Once she is comfortable with the new member of the household and is convinced that you still love her, she will relax and stop spraying.

Preventative tips Put your new pet in a separate room for the first few days, so your new pet doesn't invade your cat's territory too abruptly, and give Betsy lots of extra attention. If you are expecting visitors, sometimes it is better to put Betsy in a quiet room before company arrives so the noise and confusion won't upset her.

See also:
Strays, dealing with

Spraying, neutered male

We had our tomcat neutered so he would stop spraying, but it didn't work. He is still spraying in the house. We are going to have to get rid of him if we can't make him stop.

Why is my cat doing this? Ninety percent of male cats, even those who were dedicated sprayers, stop spraying when they are neutered. It does take some time for the hormones that triggered the spraying behavior to leave the system, so you need to allow nature to take its course.

Hoss may also be spraying in response to territorial stimuli, such as the presence of a spraying male outside the house.

How can I make him stop? Give Hoss up to two months to allow his system to be free of male hormones. Remove any environmental triggers that may be causing territorial spraying.

What to say and do Confine Hoss to an area of the house, such as the bathroom or utility room, where his spraying will not do any damage and will be easy to clean up. Go through the house and eliminate all traces of odor left from previous episodes of spraying. Use a good commercial odor remover, available from pet stores or your veterinarian, and follow the directions on the container exactly.

Putting Hoss in the bathroom will also allow you to make sure he is the one doing the spraying. Females will also spray urine as a territorial marker if there are too many cats with too little room or if a neighborhood cat is hanging out too close to the house.

Check around the outside of your entry doors and the windows to see if there are any signs they have been sprayed. If there are marks on the doors or windows, wash them off and apply the commercial odor remover. Use a commercial cat repellent, citrus peels, or cotton balls soaked in vinegar or nail polish remover to discourage neighborhood cats.

If sufficient time has elapsed and Hoss is still spraying, talk to your veterinarian about chemical intervention. There are some medications available that can help end spraying behavior.

Why this works Spraying urine is a marking device used by animals to fix the limits of their territory or to advertise their availability as sexual partners. Neutering Hoss does away with his desire to advertise, and eliminating environmental stimuli ends his need to define his territory.

Preventative tips Have your cat neutered as soon as the veterinarian says he is old enough. Male cats who are neutered before they start spraying usually never spray.

Spraying, unneutered female

My female cat has started spraying urine on the walls. She doesn't squat as she does in the litter box, but backs up to the wall just like a tomcat and squirts a stream of urine at the wall. What can I do to make her stop this?

Why is my cat doing this? Female cats use urine as sexual and territorial marking devices in much the same manner as male cats do, although the behavior is usually somewhat less frequent in females. Not all female cats spray, and those that do, spray only occasionally. This variance in frequency is because of the difference in the sexuality of the sexes. Female cats are only interested in breeding when they are in estrus, or in heat, while intact (unneutered) male cats are always interested in and available for breeding. It is fairly common for female cats in heat to spray urine on various surfaces to announce their availability. They also spray urine to mark their territory and will do so if they feel too crowded, or if there is a neighborhood cat who is invading what they consider to be their territory.

How can I make her stop? Neutering female cats is 100 percent effective in stopping sexual spraying. The surgery removes the ovaries and uterus, eliminating the hormones that trigger the desire to spray.

Territorial marking has a different origin and the environment must be changed in order to stop this type of marking behavior.

What to say and do Unless you plan to breed Daisy, have your veterinarian spay her. The surgery requires general anesthetic and usually necessitates an overnight stay in the clinic. Cats recover from the surgery with astonishing speed, and except for the stitches and bald patch on her belly, Daisy most likely will look and act like her normal self as early as the day after surgery.

If part of Daisy's problem is due to too many cats in the house, or because a neighbor's cat is invading her territory, try to reduce the stress. Put some of your cats in another part of the house for some part of the day, and rotate them through the main living area. Make sure each cat is getting enough of your attention so they don't feel left out.

Remove all traces of previous spraying episodes. Use a commercial odor remover such as Outright and follow the directions on the container exactly. Many of the more modern remedies are organic compounds and will not work if they are mixed incorrectly.

If an outside cat is crowding Daisy's territory, take steps to discourage him. Eliminate any marking he has done on the outsides of doors or windows by using the Outright. Spray around the outsides of doors and windows with a commercial cat repellent or place orange peels, lemon peels, or cotton balls soaked in vinegar or nail polish remover near the spots where you found signs of marking.

Why this works Spaying Daisy will remove any desire to advertise her sexual availability. Correcting the environmental cause of territorial spraying will end the need for her to declare her property rights.

Preventative tips Have female cats spayed as soon as your veterinarian says they are old enough, and encourage your neighbors to have their cats neutered.

Spraying, unneutered male

Our cat has started spraying very strong-smelling urine on and around both the front and back doors of the house. He is still using the litter box most of the time, but not all the time. He also occasionally urinates in the bathroom sink. How can I get him to use his litter box all the time?

Why is my cat doing this? Arthur is displaying behavior typical of a male cat entering puberty. The odor of Arthur's urine has changed because he is becoming an adult and male hormones are circulating through his system. Spraying is Arthur's method of marking his territory—telling everyone that this space belongs to him— and of advertising his availability as a sexual partner. Spraying is different from urination in that it is not done to empty the bladder. Arthur may well continue to use the litter box to relieve his bladder.

Your doorways are Arthur's territorial boundary. He sees you come and go through these doors every day and sprays them with urine to warn other male cats that they are not welcome beyond that spot.

Bathroom sinks are another favorite spot for urine marking, particularly by adolescent male cats. There is no scientific data to explain this behavior.

How can I make him stop? If done early enough, neutering Arthur will end his spraying. Cats who are neutered before they start spraying normally never start, and 90 percent of spraying males, even those who were very heavy sprayers, stop spraying after they are neutered.

What to say and do Take Arthur to your veterinarian to have him neutered—a routine and relatively simple surgery, although it requires anesthetic and your veterinarian may want to keep Arthur in the clinic overnight to make sure there are no complications. Arthur will be back to his old self, minus the spraying, in a very short time.

Arthur may continue to spray for a few days after his surgery, since it takes a while for the hormones that cause spraying behavior to be completely cleared from the system. If Arthur continues to spray, talk to your veterinarian about chemical intervention. There are medications available that help cats stop spraying.

Why this works Neutering eliminates the production of the male hormones that are the primary cause of spraying in male cats. The absence of these hormones also somewhat reduce the territorial inclinations of male cats, making them far less likely to feel the need to mark their territory by spraying.

Preventative tips Have your cats neutered as soon as your veterinarian says they are old enough. Male cats neutered before they have started spraying are unlikely ever to start.

Spraying in a new house

Ariel has always used her litter box, but since we moved into the new house she has started urinating on the carpet. She still uses her litter box most of the time, but she has three spots on the carpet that she keeps going back to. She sniffs at these spots, and if we don't catch her in time, she urinates on them.

Why is my cat doing this? Ariel is using her urine to replace another cat's territorial markers with her own. Even if the carpet was shampooed before you moved in, the scent of the urine left by the previous cat is still easily detectable by Ariel's sensitive nose. Urine is a powerful tool for marking territory, and despite the fact that the other cat is no longer around, Ariel has to eliminate that cat's scent by covering it up with her own scent. Once she has made the carpet her own by urinating on it, she will probably feel the need to refresh the markings periodically.

How can I make her stop? The odor must be completely re-moved from the carpet and Ariel must be discouraged from repeating her marking behavior.

What to say and do Use a commercial odor remover such as Outright, which is available from your veterinarian or a pet store. Follow the directions on the container exactly. Newer products are made of organic material and must be mixed exactly as directed or they will not work. If the carpet was thoroughly soaked so the urine has worked into the padding or the flooring, the carpet may have to be lifted so the areas underneath can be treated directly, or it may take several applications to completely remove the odor.

Cover the area with aluminum foil. This protects it from further soiling, and Ariel will not like the noise the aluminum foil makes when she walks or urinates on it.

Placing several dishes of cat food around the soiled area after treat-ment will further discourage her from urinating there, since cats do not like to urinate near their food. Scattering lemon or orange peels over the spots will act as a repellent, or you can use cotton balls soaked in vinegar or nail polish remover. Leave the food dishes or repellents in place for several days, replacing them as needed to assure freshness. After a few days, remove the deterrents and make sure Ariel does not return to the spot. If Ariel does return to the spot, the odor hasn't been completely removed. Repeat the application of the commercial odor re-mover and once again place the repellents over the spot.

Why this works Completely removing any trace of previous occupation by another cat eliminates the need for Ariel to do this task for herself. However, cat's noses are so sensitive that it is almost impossible to eradicate the odor to the point that it can no longer be detected. The use of aluminum foil, her food, or a repellent will help keep Ariel away from the area.

Preventative tips Immediately blot up any urine, treat the area with a commercial odor remover, and place aluminum foil and food dishes over the area.

Strays, dealing with

There is a stray cat who has been hanging around our house. We have been feeding him, but winter is coming and we worry that he will freeze to death or get hit by a car. We feel sorry for him, but we already have as many pets as we can take care of. What should we do?

What to say and do The stray may have been hiding when his owners moved. Moving day is very upsetting for family pets. They often are frightened by the excessive activity and run away or hide until the uproar is over. Unfortunately, sometimes their people can't wait for the pet to come home and finally leave without them. Other times, the people are going to a place where they can't keep a cat or they have decided they don't want a cat anymore, so they just abandon him.

Whether the neighbors left the cat behind accidentally or on purpose, he does need your help. And if he has not been neutered, he will only contribute to the overpopulation of unwanted cats. Some people think cats can fend for themselves, but that is not true. While some cats do manage to survive without much human assistance, most live brief, unpleasant lives, with constant hunger and exposure to disease and injury.

Cats are very difficult to catch unless they are very tame. If the stray cat will let you handle him, you can simply take him to the animal shelter. If the cat won't let you catch him, call your city or county animal control agency or the local humane society for help. They may lend you a live animal trap so you can humanely trap the cat and take him to the shelter.

You can also ask your local humane society to put you in contact with one of the groups that works to capture stray and abandoned cats. These volunteer workers will come to your neighborhood and, with permission from property owners, place humane traps. The cats they trap are tested for diseases, and the healthy cats are spayed or neutered and vaccinated. The volunteers will find homes for kittens and for the friendly adult cats. Unfortunately, some cats that are trapped by these volunteers have contagious diseases for which there is no cure and so must be put to sleep.

Some cats—those who have never had contact with humans or those who may have been abused—are very difficult to handle and may never be pets. Some groups place these cats, now vaccinated and neutered, back in their old neighborhoods.

Preventative tips If you are friendly with your neighbors, offer to baby-sit their cat on moving day as a good-bye gift. They might be very grateful to have the cat out from underfoot while the movers are there and appreciate being able to find him when they are ready to leave.

Sucking cloth

Our five-month-old male kitten is destroying our clothes by sucking and kneading them. He likes to suck on anything my wife and I have worn. We put our dirty clothes in a laundry hamper, but he turns the hamper over to get them. If we don't take the item away from him, he will suck on it for hours. How can we break him of this habit?

Why is my cat doing this? Usually cats who were weaned too early are the ones who continue to suck long past the age at which they should stop. Since you got Clancy when he was just six weeks old, he probably did not get enough sucking as a kitten and is trying to catch up. There is also a slight possibility that there is something missing from Clancy's diet.

How can I make him stop? Make sure Clancy's diet is adequate by feeding him a cat food approved by the American Association of Feed Control Officials (AAFCO).

Clancy has by now developed a firm habit of sucking on your clothing. It will take a determined effort to break him of this habit. If you simply put your soiled clothing out of reach, Clancy will not be cured of his sucking but will either find another target or wait until you relax your guard and allow him access to an item of clothing. You will have to restrict his access to your clothing and use taste aversion combined with on-the-spot correction using the *magazine toss* and *spray bottle* to teach him to leave your clothing alone.

What to say and do Buy a catproof laundry hamper, devise a method to latch your present hamper, or put the hamper in the bathroom or closet and close the door so Clancy can't get at it. Select one garment to sacrifice as a training tool and place it near where you sit in the evening. Gather several lightweight magazines and your spray bottle and wait for Clancy to approach the garment. As soon as Clancy puts his mouth on the garment, shout, "No, Clancy!" and use the magazine toss. Don't pick up the garment. Clancy's habit is deepseated and he will be sure to try again. This time shout, "No, Clancy! Stop it!" and use the spray bottle. Continue to bait Clancy with the garment and use the magazine toss and spray bottle until he stops approaching the garment. Repeat the exercise every evening until Clancy gives up.

Leave your designated training garment where Clancy will have access to it during the day, but make it smell bad to him. Soak cotton balls in nail polish remover and wrap the garment around them. The powerful odor will act as a repellent while you aren't there to correct him.

Why this works Clancy is long past the age when he should have been weaned. Had he been left with his mother long enough, she would have broken him of sucking sometime between six and twelve weeks of age. Mother cats usually begin the weaning process by simply moving away from the kittens when they try to nurse. Some discourage stubborn kittens by kicking them away, biting them, and hitting them with their front paws. You are substituting the mild shock of the mother's kicking or hitting with the noise of the magazine and the jet of water from the spray bottle.

Preventative tips Allow kittens to stay with their mother until they are thoroughly weaned. Kittens separated from their mothers before six weeks of age should be offered a bottle for a few weeks to allow them to get the sucking they need. Make the hole in the nipple small enough so the kitten has to suck to get his formula.

Sucking self

Our kitten sucks on her own nipple. We thought she would out-grow this habit, but she is six months old now and shows no sign that she is ready to give it up. I don't suppose it hurts anything, but we find the habit disgusting. How can we make her stop?

Why is my cat doing this? Cats who are taken from their mothers too soon, whether because something happened to the mother or because they are given to new homes, are most likely to continue sucking. It appears that kittens need a certain minimum amount of suckling, after which they are reluctantly amenable to being weaned by their mothers. This instinct to continue sucking may be nature's way of ensuring that the kittens get adequate nutrition from their mothers. There is also the psychological factor of comfort and security gained from snuggling up to their warm, purring mothers.

How can I make her stop? Wean Zora by using a combination of distraction, extra attention, and intervention. Zora's mother would have weaned her by walking away when she tried to nurse, or by pushing or kicking her away. As an active kitten, Zora would quickly have found something else to do, like play with a sibling.

What to say and do Plan to spend several weeks weaning Zora. Her habit is firmly established and will not be easy to eradicate. Supply Zora's need for psychological comfort by giving her more attention. A regularly scheduled session of petting and grooming, even as short as ten minutes, will help Zora feel secure.

When Zora starts to nurse on herself, push her head away and say, "No." Distract her with a toy, such as a ball with a bell inside, a kitty tease, or a crumpled wad of paper. Say, "Come on, Zora. Get the ball." The kitty tease (a small piece of cloth tied to a string that is attached to a fiberglass rod) is almost irresistible to cats. Drag the toy across the room or make the insect jump and fly so Zora can chase it.

Stop Zora every time you catch her sucking on herself. After pushing her head away and saying "No" a few times, start using the *hiss* to let her know you are very displeased. If you are too far away to reach her, use the *magazine toss* or *spray bottle* to startle her and make her stop.

Since Zora's sucking habit is so ingrained, you will also need to use taste aversion to help wean her. Rub the body part Zora sucks with Bitter Apple (a commercial taste repellent that can be purchased in pet stores) or with diluted vinegar or lemon juice. All of these substances lose their effectiveness after a while and need to be reapplied once or twice a day.

Why this works Physically separating Zora's mouth from what she is sucking and giving a verbal reinforcement to the action mimics what Zora's mother would have done when she weaned her. The hiss is a very strong warning to stop the behavior, and the bad taste of Bitter Apple, lemon, or vinegar also discourages this behavior. Offering Zora an exciting toy to play with simulates the type of distraction that would be provided by her siblings.

Preventative tips Leave kittens with their mothers until they are well weaned. Depending on the breed and the individual mother, this will happen sometime between six and twelve weeks. Kittens allowed to remain with their mothers generally are better at grooming themselves and have already learned to use the litter box before they go to new homes.

Toilet, drinking from

Our cat has the most disgusting habit—he drinks water from the toilet bowl. He has his own water bowl that we wash and fill with fresh water every day, but he prefers toilet water. We have chased him off the toilet many times, yelling and clapping our hands. He jumps down when we yell at him, but our efforts don't seem to make a lasting impression on him. Won't drinking from the toilet make him sick? How can we make him stop?

Why is my cat doing this? There are several theories as to why cats drink from toilet bowls. Some believe that cats like that fresh-flush taste, but that does not explain the cats who drink from the toilet in the guest bath, which is seldom used. Generally the water in their personal bowl is fresher than that in the guest toilet. Another speculation is that cats do not like to drink water that is placed too close to their food. There does not seem to be any scientific research on the subject, but anecdotal reports tell us that cats who drink from toilets will do so even if there are several water sources available to them.

How can I make him stop? It is a fact of life that cats do many things that humans find embarrassing or disgusting. One of those things is refreshing themselves at the toilet bowl. The only sure way to prevent Timothy from drinking toilet water is to deny him access.

What to say and do Cats drink water from many sources that we would consider contaminated, with no apparent ill effects. They like the dog's water, even though it is right next to his food dish; they drink from stagnant puddles, from the drip pans under plants, from rain puddles on pavement and concrete, and from the toilet bowl. While this water—which is unacceptable by human health standards—does not seem to harm cats, you need to make sure that Tim is not ingesting any harmful additives with his toilet water.

The chemicals you use to clean your toilet bowls may be harmful or fatal to Tim. Cat's systems do not filter out toxins very well, and small amounts of chemicals can cause serious illness in cats. Be sure that you carefully rinse any cleaning materials out of the bowl so Tim won't make himself sick.

If you use a continuous cleaner, one of those you place in the tank periodically, you must make sure Tim cannot drink the water. All members of the household must cooperate in an effort to make sure the toilet lid is closed or that the door to the bathroom is closed.

Preventative tips Be extremely careful with cleaning chemicals. Common household cleaners and disinfectants such as bleach, cleanser, and pine cleaners are poisonous to cats and should always be used with caution.

Reconsider whether a continuous cleaner is necessary for your household. Would you feel better knowing that the water in the toilet doesn't contain any chemicals that are potentially harmful to Tim, even though it means you have to clean the toilet periodically?

Toilet, playing in

I have always heard that cats are afraid of water or hate water, but for sure not my cat. Brandon actually enjoys playing in the water, particularly in the toilet. I don't know what he is trying to accomplish, but he seems to be trying to scoop all the water out of the toilet bowl onto the floor. He gets wet all the way up to his shoulders, and he makes a mess in the bathroom, splashing water on the toilet seat, the bath mat, and all over the floor. How can we make Brandon stop trying to empty the toilet bowl?

Why is my cat doing this? It is true that most cats dislike being wet, although no one knows why. Perhaps these fastidious creatures know how much work it takes to get a wet coat dry and back in order. When most dogs get wet, they simply shake off the excess water and let nature take its course, while cats are so concerned with their coiffure that they are unable to rest until every hair is once again dry and perfectly arranged.

Some cats are less inclined than others to avoid water, and some breeds actually seem to enjoy swimming or playing with vessels filled with water. In Turkey, the Van cat is noted for its enjoyment of swimming, and Maine Coons are notorious for playing in the water.

There are various theories about why some cats play in the water. Some people think cats are reenacting behavior their ancestors used to clear scum or marine growth off stagnant ponds so they could drink; others speculate the cats are exhibiting fishing behavior, attempting to snag (nonexistent) fish with their claws or scoop them out of the water.

Most cats are attracted to the toilet as a source of drinking water, despite the fact that their owners have provided a fresh bowl of water for them. There is no satisfactory explanation for this.

How can I make him stop? Brandon is unlikely to give up his efforts to clear the pond, catch fish, or whatever it is he is doing. This inclination to play in water seems particularly strong in some breeds, and until the instinct that causes these cats to stick their paws in the water is understood, it is unlikely that a cure can be found.

What to say and do The only defense against Brandon's fishing expeditions is to deny him access to the toilet bowl. Family members can cooperate by keeping the lid down on the toilet or by keeping the bathroom door closed.

You might provide Brandon with an outlet for his desire to play in the water by placing a large pan of water in the bathtub, where he can splash to his heart's content without soaking the floor. You might also consider moving the bath mat out of range and allowing him to continue his game, since it is relatively harmless. Keep an old towel handy for drying off the seat and mopping up the floor. If you decide to allow Brandon to continue splashing in the toilet bowl, be sure that it is free of chemicals. Do not use any of those long-term disinfectants that you drop into the toilet tank, and be sure to rinse under and around the rim of the bowl and flush several times after cleaning to remove all traces of cleaning compounds.

Why this works Knowing that Brandon is not the only cat in the entire universe who likes to play in the toilet may not make it any more fun to mop up after him, but you do have the comfort of knowing that you are not alone. Understanding that Brandon's splashing is genetic in origin might help restore your sense of humor.

Preventative tips Keep the bathroom door shut and the toilet lid closed, particularly if you use a drop-in disinfectant. Always provide Brandon with a bowl of clean, fresh water for drinking.

Toilet paper, unrolling

Our cat has a real fixation with toilet paper. If we don't keep the bathroom door closed, she will unravel the whole roll and drag it all over the house. Not only is it a nuisance to pick up, but while I'm trying to gather the paper, Trixy is right in there pouncing on it and dragging it around. It is also getting expensive. Is there any way to make her stop decorating the house with toilet paper?

Why is my cat doing this? Trixy is having a good time and burning off some of the excess energy common to all young cats. Many cats just think toilet paper is a jolly good toy, and Trixy gets double the fun by getting you to join in the game. What you think of as cleaning up her mess, Trixy views as another game—you drag the paper and she gets to chase it.

How can I make her stop? Redirecting Trixy's attention to approved toys—combined with making the toilet paper dispenser unattractive—will soon end this mischievous behavior.

What to say and do The simple solution is to block Trixy's access to the toilet paper by closing the door so she can't get into the bathroom, or installing a device to cover the paper so Trixy can't get to it. Many pet stores carry a simple, clear plastic device that fits over the toilet paper roll and prevents little paws from finding a purchase to start the unrolling process. The device is inexpensive and installation is fairly simple. The device foils would-be feline interior decorators but does not interfere with human use.

Aversion therapy works very well to teach cats to leave the toilet paper alone. Use *shaker cans* to startle Trixy so she will avoid the toilet paper, but make sure her litter box is not anywhere nearby or she may associate the shocking effect produced by the shaker cans with her litter box and stop using it, in which case you have a problem far worse than having your house decorated with toilet paper. The shaker cans are so effective that Trixy may never venture into the bathroom again.

Having made sure Trixy's litter box is in another room, balance two or three shaker cans on top of the toilet paper in the fixture (place a spare roll within reach for human use).When Trixy attacks the roll of paper she will dislodge the shaker cans, which will fall to the floor with a terrific clatter, giving her a big shock. Usually, one experience with the shaker cans is enough to discourage all but the most willful cat. However, when you hear the clatter and see Trixy shooting out of the bathroom, go in and replace the shaker cans. Leave them in place for several days until Trixy stops knocking them off.

Meanwhile, spend a little more time engaging Trixy in positive play, tossing wadded-up paper or Ping-Pong balls for her to chase, or using the kitty tease or another toy on a string. Trixy is still at the age where she has lots of excess energy she needs to run off. It is far better to help her engage in activities that charm and amuse you and help build the bond between you.

Why this works Shaker cans are especially good training tools because they allow us to do aversion training without associating us with the unpleasant activity. Cats hate to be startled. They seem to live most of their waking hours in a state of yellow alert—not quite at battle stations but keenly aware that the world is a dangerous place. Despite their calm outward appearance, most cats will jump out of their skin at a sudden loud noise. This aversion to sudden, sharp noises works to our advantage when trying to stop unwanted behavior.

Preventative tips Spend time playing with Trixy to help her run off some of her excess energy. Place toys in various locations around the house for her to find while you are gone, so her attempts to amuse herself won't result in your displeasure.

Tree, getting stuck in

I have never heard of anybody finding a cat's skeleton in a tree, and people say that the cat will come down when it gets hungry enough, but I worry about our cats. We have a lot of big old trees on our property, and I am afraid that one of them might climb too high to get back down. What would I do if one of my cats gets stuck in a tree?

What to say and do Being stuck up a tree is not a behavior problem, but you are right to be concerned. Nature endowed the cat with finely developed survival tools, which include the ability to climb trees to escape predators. The cat's claws, both front and back, are ideally shaped and positioned to give the cat a good, strong grip for climbing upward at a rapid rate. Unfortunately, cats cannot reverse their claws for coming back down. Even if the cat could figure out that it would need to be facing tail down to come down the tree, the very shape of the claw would make descent extremely difficult. The cat would have to walk its way down the tree by lifting first one paw, then another, disengaging the claws, and then digging into a lower spot on the tree. When cats dismount smaller trees, they generally dither about for quite a while and finally make an ungraceful plunge, trusting to luck that their necks won't be broken in the fall. Nor do they always land on their feet. Almost every veterinarian in the world can tell you about the cat whose jaw and/or legs were broken in a fall.

Roberta climbed up a dead sixty-foot Douglas fir and sat on the broken top for three days. Despite the chilling early spring rain that drizzled on her for three days and nights, despite the hunger pangs, Roberta was too frightened to do anything but cling to her precarious perch and cry for rescue. The tree was on a wooded lot, with no way for the fire department to bring their truck anywhere near it. The owners called a local logging outfit and inquired about having a lumberjack climb the tree with his belt and spikes. The company was kind enough to send a man to look at the situation, but climbing the dead tree, which might fall under the climber's weight, was too much of a risk. Finally a fifty-foot antenna tower was located and brought to the site. As the tower was being built, a section swung over and bashed into the dead tree, dislodging Roberta from her perch. Fortunately, the branches of the live trees surrounding the dead tree were sufficient to break her plunge to earth, and she arrived, wet, cold, hungry, and shaken—not to mention a little miffed at the abrupt nature of her descent—but apparently unharmed by her adventure. The owners subsequently had the dead tree removed.

Sapphire was missing for seven days. Her owners had combed the woods, searching and calling, when a neighbor telephoned and said she could hear a cat in the woods near her house but couldn't locate it. The owners went to the area and called Sapphire. Sapphire responded, and after ten calls and answers, they finally spotted Sapphire almost at the top of an eighty-five-foot evergreen! Certainly she must have been hungry enough to come down if she could. The owners spent a whole day trying to coax Sapphire out of the tree. Sapphire circled the tree in one direction, gingerly moving from one swaying, bouncing branch to another. She slipped, hung by one paw, and scrambled back up onto her original perch. Over and over, Sapphire circled the tree in each direction, searching for a way down, slipping, almost falling, and clawing her way back to safety. A neighborhood youth volunteered to climb the tree to rescue her but discovered the branches were much farther apart than they appeared from the ground. On the eighth day, a lumberjack came with his climbing apparatus, looked at the tree, and declared that it could not be climbed safely because of the number of branches. The safety belt would have to be unhooked and rehooked at least fifty times during the ascent and again during the descent. Luckily, the tree was so situated that the lumberjack was able to cut it down so it fell between two other trees whose limbs would check its descent. The tree fell slowly, and Sapphire dismounted about fifteen feet from the ground and ran for cover.

Where to find help The following might be able to offer assistance or suggestions: your local power and light company, tree services, logging companies, fire departments, and animal shelters. Be aware that you may have to pay a fee for assistance.

Preventative tips Keep your cat indoors where there are no tall trees, and where they won't be chased by strange animals.

Tripping

Spook is always underfoot when I am fixing dinner or every time somebody goes into the kitchen. I have tripped over him dozens of times. I think he is doing it on purpose. He never gives up, even though I have accidentally stepped on him several times. He is well fed, so he can't be doing it because he is hungry. How can I make him stay out from under my feet?

Why is my cat doing this? Spook is no dummy. What you are cooking smells wonderful, and he doesn't have to be hungry to want a taste of your delicious-smelling dinner. Spook also knows, from keen observation, that you open the refrigerator to get that wonderful-smelling food and that you store it there when you have finished your dinner.

How can I make him stop? Make it clear to Spook that he will not be rewarded for his behavior and be persistent in telling him that you do not appreciate being tripped. A cooperative family member might help by distracting Spook when you are trying to get dinner on the table.

What to say and do Never reward Spook for tripping you. Professional animal trainers use food to reinforce desired behavior, and once cats make the connection between action and reward, it is very difficult to untrain them. Once he has succeeded in earning a treat by tripping you, he will continue to repeat his trick endlessly in an effort to gain another reward. If you accidentally drop something on the floor, quickly pick it up. If Spook beats you to it, grab him and take the food away from him. Say, "No, Spook! Drop it!" and shake him by the scruff of his neck. Do not pick him up by the scruff—a grown cat is too heavy to be lifted in this manner—just grab the loose skin on the back of his neck and give a little shake. Even if he has already swallowed the tidbit, scruffing him will make the experience so unpleasant he may decide the treat wasn't worth the aftershock.

Feed Spook his regular, well-balanced diet of cat food just before you start dinner. When Spook starts winding himself around your ankles, use the *sharp clap* and push him away with your foot. Say, "No, Spook! Scram! I'm trying to cook. Get out from under my feet!" If your hands are full, use the *hiss* to let Spook know you want him gone.

An unoccupied family member can be a real boon at this time, distracting Spook with an interesting game. Have them take Spook out of the kitchen and play with him with the kitty tease or other exciting toy.

If your patience wears out before Spook does, carry him into another room and shut the door. Say, "Sorry, Spook, but you are in the way. You can come out when I'm finished."

Why this works Scruffing (grasping the loose skin on the back of the cat's neck and shaking him) is the method a mother cat uses to let her kittens know they are seriously out of line. It is a powerful method of correction and should only be used in urgent situations, such as when you need to make Spook drop something he has in his mouth.

Consistent refusal to give in to Spook's demands for a treat will eventually wear him down. Cats can be very persistent, but if you are just a little more stubborn then Spook is, he will finally give up.

The sharp clap or hiss will startle Spook and signal him that his behavior will not be tolerated.

Preventative tips Make a distinct break between the times you open the refrigerator or pantry door or fix dinner and the times Spook is given a treat. Giving him a treat right after the refrigerator or pantry door has been opened or while you are preparing dinner will quickly train him to stay underfoot.

Urinating or defecating on bed

M y cat has recently started urinating on my bed. She has always used her litter box in the past, and as far as I can tell my bed is the only place she is going outside her box. I am tired of having to wash my sheets, blankets, and bedspread. How can I make her stop this disgusting habit?

Why is my cat doing this? Cherry may be trying to tell you that she has a bladder infection. She may also be upset because you are leaving her alone more than you used to, or she may not like the new person in your life. Cats use urine as a signaling device, and anytime Cherry stops using her litter box she is making an effort to communicate with you. She may have chosen your bed as a target because she sees the bed as your territory and therefore the best place to leave a message so you will be sure to find it.

How can I make her stop? Finding the cause of the problem will help you solve it. Medical help may be needed, or Cherry may just need more attention. Take Cherry to your veterinarian and have a urinalysis done to make sure she doesn't have a medical problem. If Cherry has a bladder problem, it probably hurts when she urinates, and if the condition isn't corrected immediately, she may decide the litter box is what is causing the pain and begin avoiding it altogether.

Wash the bedding one more time. If the bedding can tolerate bleach, add some to the wash water to help remove the odor of urine. Replace the bedding and set a dish of Cherry's food over the place where she has been urinating. Keep the bedroom door closed when you aren't home.

If you have been traveling more or working longer hours, you need to convince Cherry that she hasn't lost your affection. Spend a little extra time grooming her and playing with her. While you are petting her, explain the new situation to her. Say, "I sure miss you a lot now that I am having to be out of town so much, Cherry. You are my very best friend in the whole world, and I like to be with you." Silly as it may seem, show her the calendar and tell her where you are going and when you will be back. Point to today's date on the calendar and say, "I have to leave for San Francisco today, Cherry. I'll be gone for three days, but I'll be back on Friday, this day. You are in charge while I'm gone." As you leave the house say cheerfully, "Good-bye, Cherry, see you Friday."

If a new person in your life is taking your attention from Cherry, try to include her as much as you can and make a special effort to give her extra playtime and affection.

Why this works If Cherry has a bladder problem, medical intervention will quickly end the bed-wetting episodes, and life can return to normal. If your routine has changed, Cherry just needs reassurance that she is still the most important person in your life.

Preventative tips Seek your veterinarian's services immediately at any change in litter-box habits. Catching bowel or bladder problems early makes them easier to cure and prevents bad habits from forming.

Urinating on stove or counter

I have a five-year-old spayed female that has just recently started urinating on the stove. I don't want her to get on the stove in any case, and I most certainly do not want her to use it for a bathroom. Why won't she use her litter box?

Why is my cat doing this? Marmalade either has a painful urinary tract condition or she is mad at you. Because you use the stove and counter far more often than do other household members, Marmalade has probably decided that it is your territory. Generally, when a cat urinates in an area she perceives as belonging to one person, she is expressing her displeasure with that person.

How can I make her stop? Before doing anything else, have your veterinarian rule out any medical cause for Marmalade's inappropriate toilet habit. If it hurts when Marmalade urinates, she may associate that pain with her litter box and look for a place where she can urinate without pain. Unless you act quickly, you may have serious difficulty getting her to use her litter box in the future. See if you can determine what change you have made, however trivial it may seem to you, that might have upset Marmalade. Do you have a new job that requires more travel? Is there a new person or a new pet in your life that Marmalade feels takes your attention away from her?

What to say and do Do not chastise Marmalade unless you catch her in the act. Punishment at any time will only make Marmalade resentful, and even a few seconds after the fact, she will have no idea what you are so excited about. If you catch her on the stove, use the *sharp clap* or *magazine toss* to frighten her off. Yell, "Get off the stove, Marmalade! You know you aren't supposed to be up there!" Until you discover the root of Marmalade's unsuitable choice of places to urinate, clean the stove thoroughly and cover the top of the stove with sheets of aluminum foil to keep urine off the burners. The noise she makes walking on the foil and the noise of the urine hitting the foil may in itself be enough to discourage her. Place pieces of lemon or orange peel or cotton balls soaked in vinegar or nail polish remover on top of the foil to further repel Marmalade.

Ask your veterinarian to do a complete urinalysis to make sure Marmalade does not have a physical problem. After your veterinarian gives Marmalade a clean bill of health, think for a moment what could be upsetting her. It probably is not related directly to the litter box. Cats generally need to spend less time in the litter box to urinate than to defecate. If Marmalade is still defecating in the litter box, the box itself is probably not the problem.

If there are unaltered female cats in the house, one of them may be in heat, and Marmalade feels the need to mark her territory. Unless you plan to breed your cats, have all of them neutered.

Give Marmalade some extra attention, playing with her and grooming or petting her. Say, "Marmalade, you are such a pretty girl. What a wonderful purr you have." The words don't matter—as long as "Marmalade" is used often and your tone is caressing. Even if your new schedule is frantic, both of you will feel better if you take a short break and focus your attention on Marmalade.

Why this works Urinating on the stove is a call for your attention. If Marmalade's problem is medical, relieving the pain will quickly end her need to find a comfortable place to urinate. If your job or a new friend causes her to miss your attention, the time you spend playing with and grooming her will reassure her of your affection.

Preventative tips Neuter your cat as soon as she is old enough. Feed the best-quality cat food you can find, and have regular checkups, especially as your cat grows older.

Urinating outside the litter box

My cat has stopped using the litter box. He still defecates in the box, but he urinates all over the house. His favorite spots are in the bathtub and the bathroom sink. His urine has also become very strong smelling. How can I make him go back to urinating in his litter box?

Why is my cat doing this? Willie is either telling you that he has a problem with his urinary tract, in which case you must act quickly to prevent serious illness, or he may be entering puberty and is spraying your house in order to advertise his availability to female cats. Since Willie is still using the litter box to defecate, it is unlikely that his problem is directly linked to the box itself, or to its location.

How can I make him stop? Act quickly to discover what is causing Willie to urinate outside the litter box, so you can cure the problem before the habit becomes ingrained.

What to say and do Take Willie to your veterinarian and have a urinalysis done to make sure he doesn't have an infection in his urinary tract or crystals in his urine. Left untreated, these crystals can block the urethra and lead to death. The pain caused by urinary tract disease often becomes linked in the cat's mind with his litter box. If Willie has a bladder problem, he knows only that when he squats in the litter box, he hurts.

The bathroom sink and bathtub are favorite targets of young male cats entering puberty and experiencing the first urges to spray. The change in the odor of Willie's urine indicates that he is becoming sexually mature but does not rule out the possibility of a medical problem. If your veterinarian gives Willie a clean bill of health, it is most likely that Willie is starting the territorial marking behavior common to adult male cats. If you don't plan to breed Willie, have your veterinarian neuter him. If Willie is to be used in a breeding program, you will have to confine him in an area where his spraying is easy to clean up and won't damage your furnishings.

Why this works Willie, who is naturally fastidious, would prefer to use his litter box, but he is confused by the signals he is getting from his body. Prompt attention to the cause of his problem will relieve his need to urinate elsewhere.

Preventative tips Rush your cat to the veterinarian the first time he urinates outside the litter box. Bladder conditions are very serious but can be corrected if caught early.

Have all your cats neutered as soon as your veterinarian says they are old enough.

Vomiting

M y cat doesn't seem to be sick, but she occasionally vomits. Sometimes she throws up her dinner, but usually there is just a little hair or a few pieces of what looks like grass in it; sometimes there is a big wad of what looks like hair. Sometimes she sticks her neck out and coughs before she throws up. Why is she throwing up? Is there any way to keep her from doing this?

Why is my cat doing this? There are many reasons for vomiting, such as inflammatory bowel disease, foreign bodies lodged in the digestive tract, and liver and kidney diseases, to name a few. If Moriah is vomiting more than once or twice a week, rush her to your veterinarian for a complete examination. Cats frequently eat grass when they feel the need to rid themselves of whatever is making them feel bad, so don't neglect to involve your veterinarian just because there is some grass mixed in with Moriah's stomach contents.

However, Moriah may just have a hair ball. Vomiting up swallowed hair is nature's way of keeping the hair from clogging Moriah's digestive tract. Cats of every coat length shed a little dead hair all the time, and they always swallow some of this hair during their grooming process. Usually, this small amount of hair passes harmlessly through the digestive system. The protrusions that make Moriah's tongue feel rough to you are like little combs that help her remove foreign matter and dead hair from her coat. However, the barblike protrusions face backward, and items like hair and string can't be spit out. When she is shedding heavily, Moriah swallows more hair than can be easily passed through her system, and vomiting helps her expel it. Coughing is believed to be caused by an excessive amount of hair forming into a ball and pressing on internal areas.

How can I make her stop? You can help Moriah by increasing the frequency of grooming sessions to help remove the extra hair before she licks it off and by giving her a small amount of lubricant to assist the hair in passing harmlessly through her digestive tract.

What to say and do Intensify Moriah's routine grooming sessions. If you have been combing or brushing her once a week, do so daily during the spring and summer. A good combing or brushing will remove much of the hair Moriah is shedding and help keep it out of her stomach and off your furniture. A spring bath will accelerate the loosening of dead and dying hair. Bathe Moriah and rinse her in running water an extra-long time to wash as much loose hair as possible down the drain. Stand Moriah on her hind legs by supporting her rib cage with your left hand and hold the spray nozzle against her skin, moving it in upward strokes from her hips to her shoulders. Plan to comb out loosened hair several times a day for the next two or three days.

First establish if the vomiting is due to a swallowed hair ball or a more serious digestive problem; perhaps Moriah ate something that didn't agree with her. If it is a hair ball, ask your veterinarian about giving Moriah a hair-ball remedy to help the swallowed hair pass through her digestive tract. These preparations are available from your veterinarian, pet shops, and grooming shops. They are lubricants such as petroleum jelly (with a malt flavoring to make it palatable to cats) and are sold under brand names like Petromalt, Femalt, Kittylax, Laxitone, and others. Also ask your veterinarian if a high-fiber diet would help, especially if Moriah is a little overweight.

Moriah may like the taste of the preparation enough to lick it off your finger, or you may have to use a little force. If Moriah doesn't want the remedy, you can rub it onto the roof of her mouth or rub it into the fur on the front of her leg. Smear the lubricant down the front of her leg in a fairly thin film. If you just stick on a clump of it, she will simply shake her leg and fling it across the room.

Why this works Moriah's system is just trying to stay healthy by vomiting up what can't be digested. Hair-ball remedies lubricate the hair and help it pass through the system. Helping Moriah rid herself of excess hair will prevent it from accumulating into an indigestible mass in her stomach.

Preventative tips Extra grooming during the spring and summer months will reduce the likelihood of hair balls being formed.

See also:
Hair balls

Waking, early-morning

My cat has recently started waking up earlier and earlier and demanding to be fed. I used to feed him when I got up at 7:00 A.M., but he wanted to get up at 6:00, then 5:00, and now he wants to get up at 4:00 A.M. He meows, walks on me, and licks my face until I get up and feed him. How can I make him leave me alone until I want to get up?

Why is my cat doing this? This is a bad habit and one that takes from several days to several weeks to correct.

Your cat does not obey clocks the way humans do. Since your cat can sleep all day, 4:00 A.M. seems a reasonable time to have a snack. Maybe he is a little hungry or maybe he is just bored. In any case, he has you trained to get up and provide attention or food whenever he wants.

What to say and do Change the routine and feed your cat just before you leave for work instead of immediately after you get up. In the evening, give him half of his dinner at the regular time and the rest at bedtime. Place a small dish of dry food in the bedroom so he can nibble during the wee hours. If he continues to wake you at an unreasonable hour, you must resign yourself to the fact that your cat is spoiled. When he begins his early-morning demands, say, "No, Charlie. It is too early," and push him off the bed. Be persistent. Continue pushing him off the bed, saying, "No, I want to sleep now." Do not feed him or give him any affection. Let him know that he is annoying you.

If he continues to cry and pester you, get up and put him out of the room. Carry him to the door, saying, "No, Charlie. It is too early to get up." Set him outside the door, close it firmly, and go back to bed and put the pillow over your head.

Some cats give in gracefully at this stage, but others will howl and scratch and bang on the door until you open it. This is the kitty equivalent of the child's temper tantrum. Drag yourself out of bed, pick him up, and carry him to a more distant part of the house, saying, "I'm sorry, Charlie, but I really need to sleep now. If you can't be quiet you will just have to stay in here until I'm ready to get up."

If your cat continues making enough noise to annoy other household members or your neighbors, or if his tantrums are damaging the woodwork, you must try stronger tactics. Put him in the *carrier* and put him as far away from the bedroom as possible—in the garage or basement. Say, "Charlie, people sleep at night. It is too early to get up. I need my sleep!"

On the second night, allow your cat back into the bedroom to see if he understands what you want. If he wakes you before you want to get up, push him off the bed and say, "No! It is too early to get up."

If he persists, get up, put him in the carrier, and put him in the remote spot.

Why this works Your cat likes you and wants to be near you. He also likes your soft, warm bed. Pushing him away or putting him out of the room lets him know that his behavior brings unpleasant results.

Preventative tips Don't give in! Never get up and feed your cat in the middle of the night, and don't pet him when he wakes you. When you give him what he wants, you reinforce his inappropriate behavior.

Walking on leash, resistance to

We recently bought a purebred kitten. The breeder we got her from said the kitten has to be kept indoors except under direct supervision. We would like to have the kitten go for walks with us and spend time in the garden. We tried using a leash, but the kitten doesn't like it and almost chokes herself trying to get away. Is there some way to make her stop fighting the leash and enjoy walking with us?

Why is my cat doing this? Cats are not easily taught by methods that work well on dogs. While a dog can be made to behave by jerking on its leash, cats, with their independent natures, resent the restraint and hate physical correction. Bitsy sees the leash as an affront to her dignity, and no amount of bullying will convince her to accept it.

How can I make her stop? Bitsy has to be coaxed and cajoled into doing what you want. The correct equipment, gentle introduction, and calm, cheerful instruction will help her see the benefit of walking on leash. While she may never learn to heel properly, she is still young enough to adapt.

What to say and do If you really want Bitsy to go outside, train her to wear a harness. There are several brands of harnesses designed especially for cats. Introduce her to the harness gradually. Leave the harness in a paper bag and toss it on the floor for Bitsy to examine. After the initial introduction, place the harness by her food dish. Soon the harness will be just another household furnishing. Take Bitsy on your lap and pet or groom her until she is fully relaxed. Show her the harness and say in a calm, positive voice, "Look at the pretty harness I bought for you. Isn't it pretty? This color looks very smart with your fur." Continue petting and chatting cheerfully. "Let's put the harness on, Bitsy. If you learn to walk on the harness, we can go outside together." Lay the harness across Bitsy's body and continue stroking her and talking quietly. If she doesn't make a fuss, gently slip the harness onto her. Some cats readily accept their new wearing apparel and some object. If she objects, take the harness off and try again tomorrow.

Once Bitsy has become accustomed to being in the harness, put it on her and set her on the floor. She may put on quite a show for you. If the harness fits properly—that is, if it is not too tight—it should not restrict her movements, but she will still feel it. She may flop over on her side in the broken kitty act, she may try to back out of the harness, or squirm out of it. Quickly remove the harness before she has a chance to get frustrated or panicked by it.

Gradually increase the time Bitsy spends in the harness until she finds it comfortable. When she has adapted to the point that she is wearing the harness without fuss, put her leash by her food dish and, again, allow her to become familiar with the new piece of equipment. Finally, snap the leash to the ring on the harness and let Bitsy drag it around the house.

You are ready to go outdoors. Let Bitsy lead. The reason for all this training was, after all, so she could experience the pleasure of being outdoors while you maintain enough control to keep her safe.

Why this works Cats really are pretty adaptable creatures, and if they are not forced or frightened, can be trained to do things that would not be expected of them. Many cats really enjoy their time on the leash and ask to be taken for a walk.

Preventative tips Start young and stay gentle. Kittens are more readily trained to accept a harness and leash than are older cats. Slow, gentle persuasion works best with cats. Always proceed calmly and cheerfully.

Water dish, playing in

My kitchen floor is wet all the time because my cat splashes water all over the place. He sticks his paw in his water dish and drags the dish around, slopping the water out, or he turns the dish over and spills all the water. Sometimes he dips his paw in and paddles at the water, and sometimes he dips his paw in the water and licks it. Why can't he just drink the water like a normal cat? How can I keep him from making such a mess?

Why is my cat doing this? There is no scientific data to explain the behavior of cats who play in water. There is speculation that cats who evolved in areas where the water has a lot of marine growth learned to use their paws to clear a place to drink. Others believe this is a behavior related to fishing, in which the cat is thought to be trying to snag a fish with his claws or scoop it out of the water much in the way bears fish for salmon. On the other hand, Robert may just be amusing himself.

How can I make him stop? Cats need about six to eight ounces of water a day, so fresh water should always be available for Robert. Training techniques such as scolding him or making loud noises when Robert starts to splash are not advisable in this case because they would train him to avoid the area, thereby depriving him of the water he needs. A larger container with a little less water, a heavier water dish, and a tray will help to lessen the spillage. Provide Robert with a container of water he can play in without making a mess.

What to say and do Replace Robert's metal water bowl with a heavy, quart-size pottery water dish with straight sides. The heavy pottery dish will be much more difficult for Robert to turn over. Fill the new bowl only about half full of water. When Robert splashes or drags the bowl around, the smaller amount of water in the larger dish will be less likely to spill. Use an inexpensive plastic serving tray (you can find them at housewares and hardware stores) as a place mat under the water dish. A tray will contain moderate spills and is easy to clean. Occasionally trays designed especially for pet food and water dishes are available in pet stores. These trays usually have taller sides than serving trays and are able to contain larger spills.

Provide Robert with a more acceptable outlet for his desire to play in the water. Place a large plastic or metal container of water in the bathtub for Robert's amusement. Take him into the bathroom and demonstrate your wish for him to use this source for playing. Splash the water by twitching your fingers in it and say cheerfully, "Look, Robert, here's a lovely little pond for you to play in."

Why this works Robert needs fresh drinking water for survival. Since he has to have the water and there is no way to keep him from playing in it, the next best thing is to keep spillage to a minimum and to make cleanup easier. Providing him with a container of water in an area where he can play without getting water on the floor might encourage him to use his water dish only for slaking his thirst.

Preventative tips Using larger containers and placing food and water dishes on a plastic tray reduces the amount of food and water spilled on the kitchen floor and makes daily cleanup quicker and easier.

Yowling

Our one-year-old female cat has periodic episodes of pacing and yowling. If we have a door or window open she will sit in front of the screen and yell. She sounds more like a lion than a house cat. We felt all over her to see if she has a sore spot, but we can't find anything wrong. I'm sure the neighbors think we are killing her. How can we make her stop making so much noise?

Why is my cat doing this? During the spring and summer months, it is common for female cats to become more vocal. Yowling (or calling) is one of the expressions of a female cat in heat. Maddie is advising the neighborhood male cats that she is available for mating. The amount, tone, and volume of these vocalizations vary with the individual cat, but the majority of female cats vocalize to some extent when they are in heat.

Maddie may also become excessively affectionate toward you at this time, and may exhibit other signs of being in heat, such as rolling, rubbing her face on furniture and carpets, and presenting—lowering her shoulders and treading with her hind feet with her hindquarters in the air.

While some of the premating behavior of female cats can be amusing or charming, other expressions are not so pleasing. Maddie may also use her scent to show that she is available. If Maddie has been using a scratching post, she may attack it with a great deal of vigor, both working off her frustration and covering the post with the scent from the glands in her paw pads, and she may begin clawing the furniture in an effort to broaden the areas covered with her scent. She may also start spraying urine on the walls or furniture.

How can I make her stop? Having Maddie spayed, as the surgery to remove the female reproductive organs is called, will end her need to call for a partner. Maddie's mating behavior will cease after the surgery.

What to say and do Unless Maddie is a part of a controlled breeding program, she should be spayed. If you plan to breed Maddie, consider setting aside a room in the house where she won't cause any damage in her ardor. You must exercise extreme care that Maddie does not get outside while she is in heat. Female cats can be great escape artists.

Why this works Female cats are sexually receptive only during their heat cycles. Removing the ovaries and uterus completely eliminates mating behavior in female cats. Females who are to be used in a breeding program are often confined to an area of the house where spraying and clawing won't damage anything and where surfaces are easily cleaned and deodorized.

Preventative tips If you don't plan to breed your cats, have them neutered as soon as your veterinarian says they are old enough.

Zooming, in the evening

Every night at bedtime our cat goes crazy. He zooms through the house, galloping over furniture, knocking over vases, and scattering rugs and magazines. This behavior lasts from ten to twenty minutes. Is something wrong with him?

Why is my cat doing this? This nightly discharge of energy is natural for your cat. Cats are nocturnal hunters who spend the day napping, storing up energy so they can chase their prey at night. Since you supply his food, your cat does not need to hunt to feed himself, but he still has the desire for the physical activity hunting requires. This energetic activity is an integral part of all cats' physical makeup, rather than a bad habit that needs correction.

What to say and do Since this is normal cat behavior, the easiest way to deal with it is to enjoy it. Catproof the house by moving the breakables to a spot where he cannot harm them during his nightly romp and join in the fun. Laugh and applaud his antics. Say, "Attaboy, Eddie—Nice jump! Go, go, go, Eddie!"

Alternately, you can direct his energy into other forms of play. Playing with your cat will help him diffuse his excess energy without destroying your valuables. Cats hunt small rodents and birds, so their hunting technique consists of running in short bursts, lunging, and leaping high into the air. You can simulate the activities of prey for him with a variety of inexpensive toys. Small sponge balls or crumpled paper make excellent prey and are small and light enough for him to carry after he catches them. You can make paper ball chasing even more exciting for your cat by crinkling the paper between your fingers, causing it to make "prey" noises before you throw it, and saying, "Eddie, Eddie! Get the mouse. Where's the mouse, Eddie? Get it!" Cats love this activity, and some even learn to fetch, bringing the toy back over and over. Be inventive. There are dozens of low- and no-cost toys you can make, such as a cardboard box with a jingle ball inside, or a paper grocery bag with the top folded over to keep it open. Place the bag on its side and scratch on the end. Your cat will probably dive into the bag and attack the "mouse" (your finger).

Tie a small toy to a string and drag it for him, giving both of you some exercise, or purchase a kitty tease, a small piece of denim on a string attached to a small fishing pole. The kitty tease will allow you to give your cat a good, tiring workout while you sit, casting and dragging the lure. Your cat can be teased into leaping quite high in pursuit of the prey. Be sure to store any toys with strings in a drawer or closet where he can't play with them without your supervision.

Why this works The workout your cat gets from playing with toys will fulfill his instinct to chase and lunge at prey. The toys become the prey and your cat gets to pretend he is the hunter-killer his wild ancestors were.

Preventative tips Get in the habit of playing with your cat every day so he will get lots of exercise.

Appendix

Clipping Claws

If you are nervous about clipping your cat's claws, have a professional groomer, your veterinarian, or your veterinarian's technician demonstrate the technique for you. Knowing the proper technique will help you and the cat relax and make the job easier on both of you.

Buy a pair of nail clippers designed just for cats. Human nail clippers can be used, but having the right equipment makes the job easier and reduces the danger of accidentally injuring your cat by nipping her paw pad or pulling the hair around her toes.

Place your cat on your lap with her head pointed away from you. Extend her claw by gently lifting her paw and pressing the pad with your index finger while pulling back gently with your thumb on top of the paw. Don't hold your cat's paw with any more force than is necessary to position the claw for clipping—cats do not like to have their paws held, and too firm a grip will make her want to escape. Look to see where the pink vein ends just before the curve of the claw. Place the clipper outside of the vein and snip the tip off the claw.

It is helpful to have an assistant distract your cat by gently scratching her ears and chin or by dangling a string or toy in front of her while you work.

Praise your cat throughout the session, saying, "Oh, you are such a brave kitty! What a nice girl to sit still while we make your feet pretty!"

If your cat is very uncooperative, don't turn the first session into a battle of wills—forcing your cat will make subsequent sessions more difficult. Stroke her with one hand and talk gently to her while you fondle her paw with the other hand. When she has relaxed, let her get down, then try again later. A slow, gentle approach will help her understand that no harm comes from what you are doing. After she has become accustomed to having you handle her paws, just clip

Having the proper tool makes the job easier. Claw clippers like these are available at most pet stores.

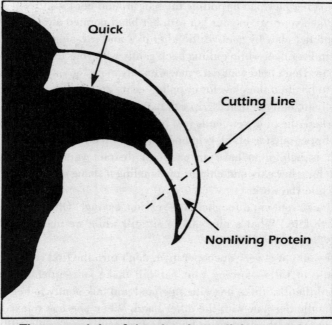

Quick

Cutting Line

Nonliving Protein

The curved tip of the claw is nonliving protein, which appears clear or white in most cats. The pink area is the quick, which contains nerves and blood vessels. Clip below the pink area.

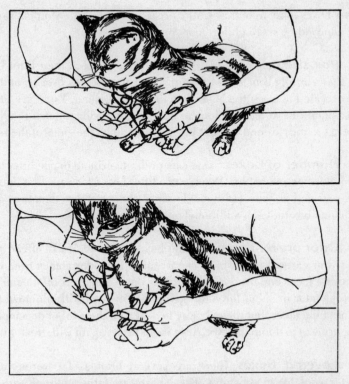

Hold the paws gently but firmly. Press up on the paw pad with your index finger and press down and back with your thumb to extend the claw. Place the notch in the claw clippers at the top of the curve in the claw and clip off the end.

one or two claws at each sitting. When you have finished the session, give her a treat to reward her bravery.

Litter-Box Care

The majority of litter-box problems can be prevented by supplying litter boxes that are large enough for your cats and enough boxes for the number of cats you have, and by keeping them clean. Place your litter boxes away from high traffic areas and make sure your cat won't be annoyed by small children or your dog.

Box size Cats need to be able to turn around in their litter box so they can dig a hole and then position themselves over it, and to turn around to cover the hole when they are finished. Your cat's litter box should be at least as long as your cat and wide enough to allow the cat to turn around without having to stand on the sides of the box.

Number of boxes Some cats prefer to urinate in one litter box and defecate in another. Provide two litter boxes for your first one or two cats and provide additional boxes if you have more than two cats. Add one box for each additional one to two cats.

Odor prevention If the litter box smells bad, it will offend you and your cat will not want to use it. Litter-box odor comes from two sources: feces and urine, which breaks down and gives off an ammonialike odor in about three days. Top-quality food will minimize the odor of the feces, but the only way to deal with the odor of decomposing urine is to dump the box, rinse it, and start again with fresh litter.

Covered boxes There are several brands of covered litter boxes available in pet stores. These boxes are fully enclosed, with an opening in one end for the cat to go in and out. The box and cover are actually two pieces, which can be taken apart for cleaning. Covered litter boxes will reduce the amount of litter that gets thrown out of the box during digging and will give your cat some privacy, but they will not eliminate cat-box odor from your home—only keeping the box clean will keep it from smelling bad. The problem with covered boxes is that you can't see that the box needs cleaning, and the lid may keep you from smelling any odor until it gets very strong, so you might forget to clean it. You will have to develop a routine to make sure the box is kept clean.

Clumping-type litter Clumping-type litter absorbs moisture and forms lumps that are easy to scoop out and remove from the box.

Because most of the urine is trapped, this type of litter has a longer box life than clay litter, but it will eventually start to smell bad and need replacing. Sniff the box occasionally to make sure it still smells fresh.

Tracking and scattering litter Place your cat's litter box inside an upside-down cardboard box with one end cut out. The high sides of the box will give your cat some privacy and will keep the litter from being scattered if your cat is an enthusiastic digger. Place a small rug or towel in front of the box to catch the litter that clings to your cat's feet.

Eliminating odor Start with a clean litter box filled with fresh litter to a depth of one to two inches. Scoop out solids every day and empty, rinse, dry, and refill the box once a week or when one third of the litter is wet. Dump soiled litter into a plastic bag, tie the top, and place it in the garbage. Scrub the box with soap and water, rinse thoroughly, dry, and refill with fresh litter.

New Kitten

New kittens can be overwhelmed. They are taken away from all that is familiar—home, furnishings, mother, siblings, and people—and are thrust into a totally new environment. The stress of the move often brings on sniffles, sneezes, and watery eyes, or mild to severe diarrhea. If the condition persists for more than three days, or if the discharge from his eyes or nose becomes yellow or green, or his stool becomes bloody or watery, take him to your veterinarian. Do as much as you can to minimize the changes for the kitten. Ask the person you are getting him from if you can borrow a familiar toy or some bedding from his old home to help ease his move, and provide him with the same brand of food he has been eating.

Before you bring your new kitten home, choose a small room (usually the bathroom) where he can be confined for a few hours while he recovers from the trauma of the car ride. Put his food and water, litter box, and scratching post in that room.

When you arrive home, take your kitten to his room, open the carrier door, and allow him to come out when he is ready. Give him a chance to relax before he has to start adjusting to new family members. Take turns visiting the kitten. Have family members enter the room quietly, saying, "Hello, baby, how are you doing?" and sit and talk quietly to him for a few minutes. It doesn't matter much what you say—you are just letting him learn the sound of new voices and showing him that he has nothing to fear from you.

After your kitten has eaten his food and used the litter box, you can open the door so he can explore on his own. If you allow him to walk out of the room, rather than carry him, he will always be able to find his way back to the litter box.

Remember that your kitten has very short legs and a small bladder. You may need to provide several litter boxes so he doesn't find himself too far from the toilet when he needs to use it.

If you have other cats, allow several days for them to become used to each other before you allow the kitten out of confinement. Allow them to sniff each other through the closed door until your resident cat stops hissing and growling. Give your resident cat extra affection, grooming, and play sessions to reassure her that she is not being replaced.

It is normal for your resident cat to show your new kitten who is boss in the house by growling, hissing, and swatting him. As long as your resident cat is not seriously beating up on your kitten, allow them to work things out on their own. If your resident cat gets too rough with the kitten, put the kitten back in the bathroom and try again the next day. Cats adjust to change slowly, but your resident cat should be tolerating the kitten within a few days, and if you allow them to proceed slowly, they should eventually become friends.

Poisons

The National Animal Poison Control Center advises that your cat's system is not designed to deal well with toxic substances. Many substances that are beneficial to humans when taken in small doses, such as aspirin, can be deadly poisons to cats. Many automotive and gardening chemicals, such as antifreeze and snail bait, are not only poisonous but are also very attractive to cats. Antifreeze is such a hazard to pets because of its attractive, sweet taste; you should consider switching to the nontoxic Sierra brand. Store all medications and household, automotive, and garden chemicals out of your cat's reach and promptly wipe up any spills. Do not give your cat any medication unless directed to do so by your veterinarian.

If you think your cat has ingested a toxic substance, call your veterinarian or, if he or she is not available, the National Animal Poison Control Center (NAPCC). There is a fee for NAPCC's services. You can have the fee charged to your credit card by calling 1 (800) 548-2423.

Toxic Houseplants

Aloe vera and true aloe
Apple
Apple leaf croton
Apricot
Asparagus fern
Autumn crocus
Avocado
Azalea
Bird of paradise
Branching ivy
Buckeye
Buddhist pine
Caladium

Calla lily
Castor bean
Ceriman
Christmas rose
Diffenbachia
Dracaena
Dragon tree
English ivy
Holly
Hurricane plant
Indian laurel
Indian rubber plant
Japanese yew
Jerusalem cherry

Kalanchoe
Lily of the valley
Marble queen
Marijuana
Mistletoe "American"
Morning glory
Mother-in-law
Narcissus
Pothos
Philodendron
Rubber plant
String of pearls/beads
Weeping fig

Index

About the Author

ALICE RHEA is a judge for The International Cat Association (TICA). She handles hundreds of cats during each cat show and has judged shows across the United States and in Canada, France, and South America. Alice breeds and shows Maine Coon cats, and has consistently produced award-winning cats. Alice has been training cats and counseling cat owners for over ten years. Most cat owners can easily deal with their cat's behavior problem with simple over-the-phone instruction, but occasionally a home visit is needed to demonstrate nail clipping or bathing techniques for especially nervous owners. Alice also visits nursing homes with cats and kittens to allow patients to enjoy the pleasure of petting cats and watching kittens play. As the Washington State Feline Chair for the Morris Animal Foundation, Alice helps raise funds to support medical research for the benefit of cats.

Alice also writes for her local newspaper and won the 1993 and 1994 Washington State Publishers' Association award for investigative reporting, and she is the editor of *TICA Trend*, a magazine exclusively for cat breeders and exhibitors.

Alice and her husband live in rural King County near Seattle, Washington, with ten Maine Coon cats, two mixed-breed cats, five Alaskan Malamutes, and a Border Collie.